D5 Erweiterte Ausgabe

English G 21

Klassenarbeitstrainer

für Schülerinnen und Schüler

mit Lösungen
Lerntipps

W0320822

Vokabel Trainer
Cornelsen

Vokabeltrainer-App

Verfügbar für: iOS, Android und Windows Phone

scook

AUDIOS online

Deine **Audios** findest du hier:

1. Gehe auf scook.de.
2. Gib den unten stehenden Zugangscode in die Box ein.
3. Hab viel Spaß mit den Audios.

Dein Zugangscode auf
www.scook.de | g8ydq-4vs4z

Cornelsen

English G 21 • Band D5 Erweiterte Ausgabe

Klassenarbeitstrainer mit Lösungen und Lerntipps

Konzeption
Dr. Ursula Mulla und Nogi Mulla, Germering

Erarbeitet von
Bärbel Schweitzer M.A., Staufen

In Zusammenarbeit mit der Englischredaktion
Dr. Christiane Kallenbach (Projektleitung)
Gwendolyn Düwel (verantwortliche Redakteurin), Ulrike Berendt
Susanne Bennetreu, Stefanie Juhnke (Bildredaktion)

Beratende Mitwirkung
Helge Kipp, Mülheim an der Ruhr
Martina Schroeder, Stedtlingen

Tonaufnahmen
Clarity Studio Berlin

Illustrationen
Constanze Schargan, Berlin (S. 8; 11; 19; 20; 26)

Bildquellen
Alamy, Abingdon (S. 14 unten: Gerry Walden; S. 21 unten li.: moodboard; S. 27: Robert Dant; S. 29 Bild 3: imagebroker, Bild 4: Image Source; S. 34 oben: OJO Images Ltd, Mitte Mitte: Image Source; S. 36: Russell Kord; S. 38: Design Pics Inc. (RF); S. 41: Myrleen Pearson; S. 42: Glyn Thomas Photography); **Corbis**, Düsseldorf (S. 4 Mitte: Reuters / Darren Staples; S. 14 oben: Robert Harding World Imagery / Claire Leimbach; S. 21 oben re.: Bernd Vogel; S. 47 li.: Dave Bartruff, re.: Radius Images (RF); S. 53: Jim Craigmyle; S. 56 unten: Hugh Sitton); **Getty Images**, München (S. 12 Bild 2: Grant Faint; S. 34 Mitte re.: Photographer's Choice RF / Rayman (RF); S. 35: Cultura / Echo (RF); S. 61: Andreas Stirnberg); **iStockphoto**, Calgary (S. 4 re.: Sara Winter, 2. v. li.: David Freund; S. 7: Sara Winter; S. 12 Bild 3: Warwick Lister-Kaye, Bild 4: Linda Kloosterhof; S. 24: Rubberball; S. 30 unten re.: Kemter, unten li.: Steve Cole; S. 32: Loretta Hostettler; S. 37 oben: kate_sept2004; S. 43 li.: David Sucsy, Mitte: snapphoto; S. 54 oben: majana; S. 57: Petko Danov); **Photolibrary**, London (S. 29 Bild 1: Corbis, Bild 2: White / DV; S. 30 oben: Bridge / Ansgar Ansgar); **Picture Alliance**, Frankfurt/Main (S. 12 Bild 1: Lonely Planet Images; S. 37 unten: Photo Alto; S. 39: dpa; S. 48: Arco Images GmbH); **Moritz Schweitzer**, Villingen-Schwenningen (S. 5); **Shutterstock**, New York (S. 4 li.: Taras Vyshnya, 2. v. re.: markrhiggins; S. 10 li.: Paul Coartney, re.: John Carnemolla; S. 17: Coprid; S. 21 oben li.: Ioannis Pantzi, unten re.: Yuri Arcurs; S. 34 Mitte li.: hightowernrw, unten: Stephen Coburn; S. 40: 2happy; S. 43 re.: Goodluz; S. 47 Mitte: Kuzma; S. 54 unten: Tommaso79; S. 56 oben: MikeE; S. 62: Marko Tomicic)

Titelbild
Alamy, Abingdon (Henry Westheim Photography); **Corel Library** (flag Hintergund (M))

Layout und technische Umsetzung
Heike Freund, Hameln

Umschlaggestaltung
Klein und Halm Grafikdesign, Berlin

www.cornelsen.de
www.EnglishG.de

1. Auflage, 4. Druck 2020

Druck: H. Heenemann, Berlin

ISBN 978-3-06-032326-5

PEFC
PEFC/04-31-1156

PEFC zertifiziert
Dieses Produkt stammt aus nachhaltig bewirtschafteten Wäldern und kontrollierten Quellen.

www.pefc.de

INHALT

Schon wieder eine Klassenarbeit …

Liebe Schülerin, lieber Schüler,
wer sich gut vorbereitet, kann der nächsten Klassenarbeit gelassen entgegenblicken. Der Klassenarbeitstrainer unterstützt dich ganz gezielt beim Üben für alle Klassenarbeiten. Du findest zu jeder Unit zwei Klassenarbeiten, mit denen du alle Fertigkeiten (skills) trainieren kannst, die du für die Klassenarbeiten benötigst.

Einige Tipps für ein erfolgreiches Lernen mit deinem Klassenarbeitstrainer:

Vorbereitung
Informiere dich genau über die Inhalte der kommenden Klassenarbeit. In einem Lernplan legst du fest, welche Aufgaben du an welchem Tag bearbeiten willst. Plane dazu genügend Zeit ein. Bei Unklarheiten solltest du zuerst im Englischbuch nachsehen. Erst wenn du hier nicht weiter kommst, holst du dir Hilfe von anderen. Am Tag vor der Arbeit wiederholst du nur kurz.

Inhaltsverzeichnis
Im Inhaltsverzeichnis kannst du ablesen, welche Kompetenzen pro Klassenarbeit geübt werden. Oft gibt es auch zwei unterschiedliche Aufgaben zu einer Kompetenz, z.B. zum Listening oder zum Writing. Wähle eine aus oder löse beide Aufgaben.

Lernheft
Führe ein Heft für Schreibaufgaben und zusätzliche Übungen. Achte auf Übersichtlichkeit (Datum, Überschrift, Aufgabe, Seite). Lege auf der ersten Seite ein Inhaltsverzeichnis an. So kannst du bei Unklarheiten immer wieder nachschlagen. Es hilft dir auch, wenn du eine Aufgabe wiederholen möchtest.

Lösungsheft
Vergleiche deine Lösungen mit den möglichen Lösungen. Sieh dir dabei deine Fehler ganz genau an und analysiere sie. Nur so kannst du aus deinen Fehlern lernen. Im Lösungsheft findest du Lerntipps mit weiteren Übungen und auch die Hörtexte.

Punkteschlüssel
Bei jeder Klassenarbeit ist die Gesamtpunktzahl für alle Aufgaben angegeben. Solltest du beim Lernen eigene Schwerpunkte setzen und deswegen Aufgaben weglassen, musst du die Gesamtpunktzahl neu ermitteln. Mit dem Punkteschlüssel kannst du deine Leistung einschätzen.

Übrigens: Die Klassenarbeiten in diesem Heft prüfen das Gelernte sehr ausführlich ab.
Du brauchst daher für die Bearbeitung länger als eine Schulstunde.

Jetzt kann es aber wirklich losgehen – **let's get started!**

All the best,

Bärbel Schweitzer

Gesamtpunktzahl ohne Speaking	_____ / 98	Note	_____
Gesamtpunktzahl mit Speaking	_____ / 119	Note	_____

LISTENING

_____ / 17

01 1 A high school photo competition

_____ / 12

There has been a photo competition at a high school in Australia. Mrs Miller and Mr Bush, the two art teachers, and Lesley, a student, are going to make the final decision about the winning photograph.

a) *Look at the photos, then listen to the discussion and write the correct number in the boxes. (6P)*

A

B

C

D

E

F

b) *Listen to the text again. Then tick the correct statement about each photo. (6P)*

Number 1	a) This is Lesley's favourite photo.	
	b) Lesley knows where the photo was taken from.	
	c) The photo shows Sydney from the north.	
Number 2	a) Mr Bush thinks this is the best photo.	
	b) They can't choose this photo because it's from a postcard.	
	c) Mr Bush knows the place on this photo.	
Number 3	a) The photo could also be from of country.	
	b) Mr Bush would like to walk on the lonely pier.	
	c) Lesley does not like the colours.	
Number 4	a) The clouds in number 4 are not so nice.	
	b) Mr Bush likes number 4 more than number 5.	
	c) There is not much movement in the photo.	
Number 5	a) Mrs Miller's hobby is sailing.	
	b) The blue sky is fabulous.	
	c) The photo could also be of another country.	
Number 6	a) The photo shows a view that they haven't seen before.	
	b) The Harbour Bridge is on the right.	
	c) Mr Bush thinks this is the best photo.	

02 2 An interview for the school radio station

___ / 5

Listen to Maya and Steve on the Caroline Chisholm High School radio. Then complete the mind map.

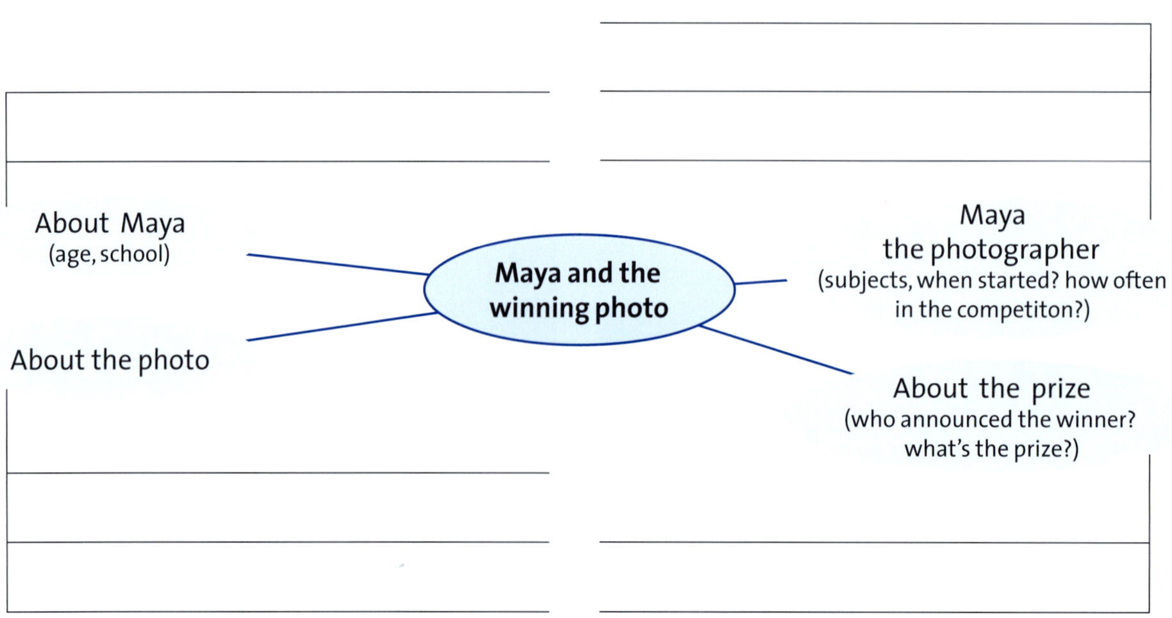

LANGUAGE

___ / 30

1 WORDS A report about the photos

___ / 7

Complete the text with words from the box. Be careful: There are three more words than you need. Make sure you use the correct form of the nouns and the verbs.

because of • wave • desert • witness • surprising • (to) avoid • at someone's place • recent • reef • nearly • nowhere • advice • barbecue • outdoors • percentage • (to) get married • (to) divide sth. (into)

It was ______________ that so many people were interested in the photo competition. We received more than 200 photos from 152 students. We ______________ the photos into different groups. ______________ half of the photos were of Australian natural sights: the blue sea with the high ______________, the fish that live in the ______________ or animals that can only be found in Australia. A high ______________ of the photos show Australian everyday life: a party ______________, people spending their free time ______________, a ______________, at the beach. One photo even shows a young couple ______________ at the beach in Sydney. There are others of the beautiful Australian ______________. ______________ the number of photos, we had to organize three rounds to find the winner.

For the last round we invited the art teachers to help us make our decision. They gave us important ______________ on how to choose the best photos. It wasn't easy. We wanted ______________ choosing a photo which looked like the famous pictures of Australia which all the tourists know, but the choice was just so large!

2 GRAMMAR A day in Maya's family

____/11

a) *Maya has taken photos of a normal day in her family.*
Describe what the members of her family do everyday. Choose words from the box. Use the ***simple present****. (8P)*

(to) catch the bus to school • (to) do homework • (to) come home from work • (to) get up • (to) go to work • (to) have breakfast • (to) have tea • (to) read books • (to) watch TV

My mum and dad

We all

Sue and I

My mum

My mum

Sue and I

We all

My mum and dad / Sue and I

1 *My mum and dad get up at 7.15 every day.*

2 *We all* ____.

3 ____.

4 ____.

5 ____.

6 ____.

7 ____.

8 ____.

b) *Now write two sentences about what you usually do and one about what you don't do on week days.*
Use your exercise book. (3P)

3 GRAMMAR Maya is this year's winner

____ /7

*The following text is taken from the school magazine. Complete the text. Use the **simple past**.*

In 2000 our school ____________________ (start) organizing photo competitions once a year.

Every year there ____________________ (be) a happy winner.

This year in April the students ____________________ (have to) hand in their photos. Like every year you ____________________ (can) take part with one or more photos. A team of art teachers and students ____________________ (look) at all the photos and ____________________ (choose) the best eight.

That ____________________ (be) hard work, says Lesley, one of the students.

Still, they ____________________ (manage) to do it and they finally ____________________ (have) just six photos to choose from. Of course, they ____________________ (not know) the names of the students who had taken them.

The last round ____________________ (be) the hardest because all the photos ____________________ (be) really brilliant. In the end we ____________________ (pick) one photo which ____________________ (look at) this year's topic in a very special way. Congratulations to Maya.

4 GRAMMAR The morning before the announcement

____ /5

*Maya talks about the day when the winner was announced. Use the **simple present** and **simple past**.*

Last Thursday I ____________________ (be) terribly nervous because I ____________________ (know) that the winner of the photo competition would be announced at lunch break.

I usually ____________________ (not like) getting up early in the morning, but last Thursday I ____________________ (be) the first in the bathroom. And I ____________________ (have) time to enjoy a really good breakfast. A fantastic start to an exciting day! Every day after morning lessons I ____________________ (spend) some time chatting with my friends. But last Thursday I ____________________ (go) to the assembly hall right away.

When the art teacher ____________________ (say) my name, I ____________________ (can not) believe my ears at first. But after the first shock everything ____________________ (turn out) to be fine.

MEDIATION

____ / 31

1 A photo competition

____ / 11

The following text is taken from the Australian magazine 'The one and only Australia' which has started a photo competition.

'The one and only Australia' monthly photo competition

We love everything that's special, wonderful and unusual about Australia.
And we love seeing what you like about our country too. This month the topic of our photo competition is

One moment in Sydney

Enter our competition and you could win a $500 camera!

How to enter:
When you have chosen your photo, write a short description of it.
You should also give details of when and where the photo was taken.
You should send your name, your full address and telephone number and a caption with the photo.
Photos must be at least 1 MB in size.

Some rules:
The closing date for your entry is October 10 at midnight.
The competition is open to everybody aged 16 and over.
Each person is allowed to hand in one photo only. Of course you can take part again next month!

Send your photo by e-mail to:
photocompetition@theoneandonlyaustralia.au

Please note that letters (with photos) sent by post will not be accepted in the competition.

The winner:
The winner's photo will be published in our magazine next month together with his or her name.

Think you've got a winning photo? We're waiting to see it!

Einer deiner Freunde ist ein guter Fotograf und möchte an diesem Wettbewerb teilnehmen. Hilf ihm, den Text zu verstehen. Schreibe deine Lösung in dein Lernheft.

Teile ihm mit ...
1. welche Vorgaben es für die Fotos gibt (sieben Dinge)
2. die Teilnahmebedingungen (mindestens vier)
3. den Preis
4. wann ein Foto nicht zum Wettbewerb zugelassen wird
5. was geschieht, wenn man mit einem Foto gewonnen hat (zwei Dinge)

2 In the shop

____ / 20

*Julia is an exchange student from Germany in Maya's class. She wants to buy a new camera. Maya goes shopping with Julia to help her choose the camera. Take **Maya's** part.*

Julia Danke, dass du mit mir in den Laden gehst. Bei solchen Einkäufen fühle ich mich mit meinen Englischkenntnissen noch nicht sicher genug.

Assistant Hello you two. How can I help you?

Julia OK. Sag ihm, dass ich einen neuen Fotoapparat kaufen möchte, weil mein alter nicht mehr funktioniert.

Maya ______________________________ (2P)

Assistant What kind of camera would you like to buy?

Maya ______________________________ (1P)

Julia Sag ihm doch, dass ich eine Kamera suche, die gute Fotos macht und dennoch nicht so teuer ist.

Maya ______________________________ (2P)

Assistant OK, I understand, I can show you some good cameras. Just a minute.

Maya ______________________________ (1P)

Assistant Here you are: this X 400 is a good camera. Take a look at the display. It's quite large.

Maya ______________________________ (3P)

Julia Mir gefällt die Kamera. Fragst du bitte, wie viel sie kostet.

Maya ______________________________ (2P)

Assistant It's $450.

Maya ______________________________ (1P)

Julia Frag mal, ob er noch andere ähnliche Kameras hat, die er uns zeigen kann und die nicht ganz so teuer sind.

Maya ______________________________ (2P)

Assistant Here's one for $350. The quality is nearly the same but it's not as light and the display is smaller.

Maya ______________________________ (3P)

Julia Also, ich glaube, es ist die richtige Kamera, ich nehme sie.

Assistant OK, I've already understood. It's a good choice. Let me give you an extra battery as a present.

Maya ______________________________ (3P)

Maya That's very kind of you, thank you very much. Bye-bye.

Julia Bye!

WRITING

____ / 20

Young Australians and animals

You are one of the members of the jury in a photo competition. You are asked to give your opinion about the four photos above and to say which of the photos you like best.

- Start with one or two opening sentences about the photos.
- Give some information about each photo.
- Choose your favourite photo.
- Describe it in detail and give reasons why this is your favourite one.
- Write about 130–150 words in your exercise book.

SPEAKING

____ / 20

03 Charts about the competition

A group of students has collected some statistics about the photo competition. Look at the chart and listen to Sara.

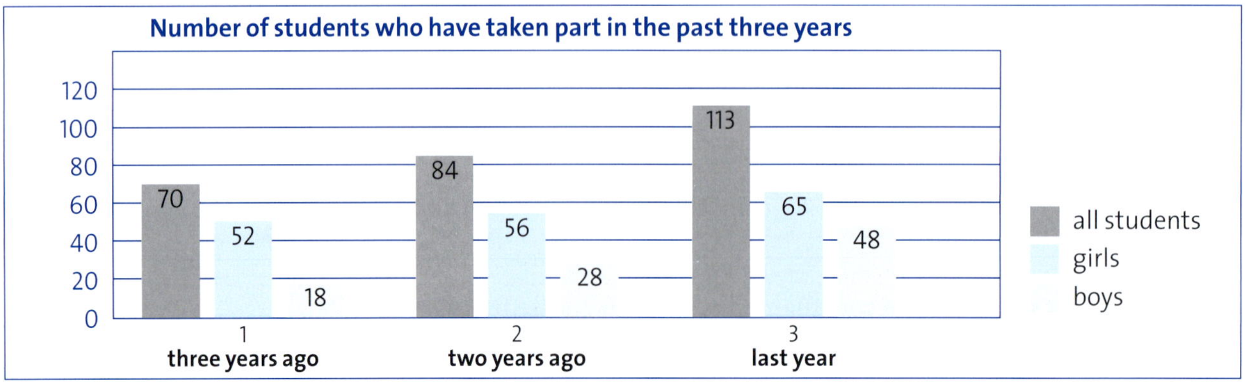

Now you

Look at the bar charts below and explain them. Say what the two charts show, give details and finish with a conclusion. Before you start speaking, make some notes.

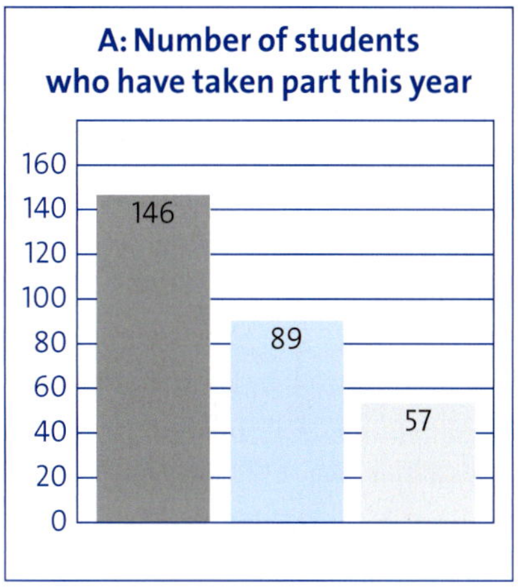

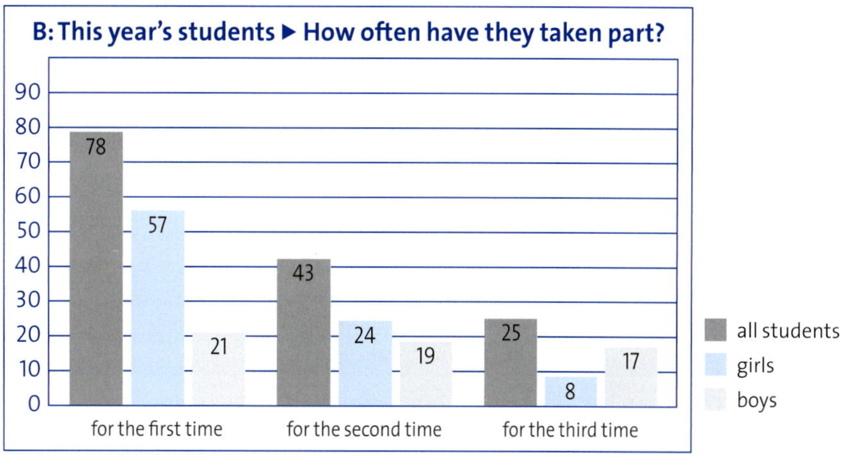

Statistiken
- Diese Übung passt zum Skills File auf S. 140 und zur Übung auf S. 10 in deinem Englischbuch.
- Informationen über Statistiken enthalten meist die drei Teile:
  1. Informationen darüber, was die Statistik zeigt: *The bar chart shows ...*
  2. Genaue Beschreibungen und Erklärungen: *The bar chart compares the number of ...*
  3. Schlussfolgerungen: *So ..., you can say that ...*
- Gliedere deine Erklärungen, indem du in die Tabellen unten deine Stichpunkte einträgst.
- Wenn du mehr sprachliche Hilfen benötigst, schau auf S. 10 im Lösungsheft nach.

Chart A

1 What the chart is about	
2 Details about the chart	
3 My conclusions	

Chart B

1 What the chart is about	
2 Details about the chart	
3 My conclusions	

You can start like this:

Welcome to my presentation about about the number of students who entered the photo competition this year. The first chart shows that there were ... / The second chart looks at how often students take part in the competition. It shows in detail how many ...

Klassenarbeit B

Gesamtpunktzahl ______ / 64 Note ______

READING

______ / 12

Some special information for tourists in Australia

from "Australia for you", your special tourist office

For most tourists buying souvenirs is an important way to remember their holiday trip. We know that the didgeridoo is often at the top of tourists' shopping lists when they come to Australia. *Australia for you*, your special tourist office, wants to offer you some help in finding your very own digeridoo.

Do you want to take a didgeridoo home with you? Here's the information you need.

1

There are different stories about the first didgeridoo. Too many, really. Only one thing is sure: the didgeridoo is one of the oldest instruments in the world. We know that originally it was a musical instrument played by the North Australian Aborigines. It's an important part of Aboriginal culture and is played mostly by men. The player tries to imitate the sounds of nature in the Australian outback: the animals, the plants, the wind, running water …

2

Did you know that a didgeridoo is made by insects? They live in Eucalyptus trees and eat the inside of the tree's branches. The hollow[1] piece of wood is used to make the didgeridoo. Of course, the insects are taken out of the inside first!

3

Tourists often ask this question once they know that the hole in a didgeridoo is not man-made. It sounds easy to make a didgeridoo yourself, but really it's a long process. First of all, you have to look for and find the correct piece of wood. That's the most difficult part because it's got to be a living tree with hollow branches. The trees are cut, they are cleaned on the inside, and the bark[2] has to be taken off. Didgeridoo makers then use different tools to tune the instrument. Finally, the outside is painted beautifully. A mouthpiece is added.

4

Of course, you want a real Aboriginal product, but that's not an easy job. Some didgeridoos are not made from Eucalyptus. You may find didgeridoos made of plastic. You might also find didgeridoos that were made abroad. You won't be happy with one of those. You should look around the Aboriginal arts and crafts or instrument shops until you're sure you're buying a real Aboriginal product. No matter which Aboriginal product you buy, you should always support the Aboriginal culture.

5

There are didgeridoo schools all over Australia, both in cities and in the country. One thing you need to know before you start: you'll need time and practice. So look out for a beginners course that helps you with your first steps. You have to learn how to breathe through your nose and out through your mouth at the same time. Make sure you're taught these techniques at the beginning. You should go on practising in your home country. There are also free internet websites with movies that help you practise.

**Have fun with your didgeridoo.
It's the sound of Australia.**

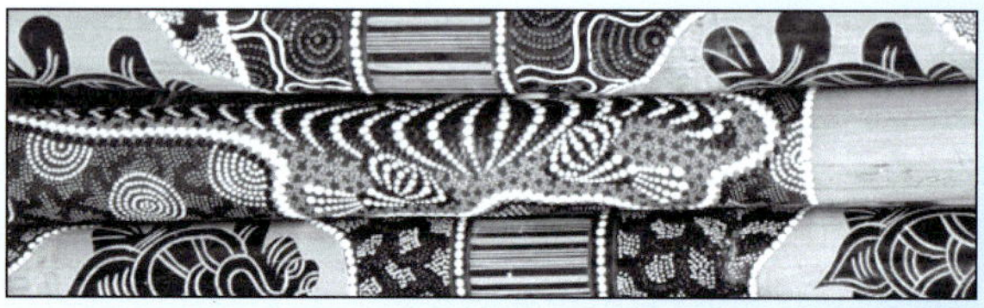

[1] hollow branch ['hɒləʊ brɑːntʃ] *hohler Ast*   [2] bark [bɑːk] *Borke, Rinde*

1 Missing headings

____ / 5

Match the headings to the paragraphs 1–5. Be careful: There are two more headings than you need.

A Can I learn to play the didgeridoo?
B Can I make a didgeridoo myself?
C What is a didgeridoo?
D One of the oldest instruments
E How can I find the right didgeridoo?
F Didgeridoos and other instruments
G Tourists and didgeridoos

1		2		3		4		5	

2 About the text

____ / 7

Answer the questions with information from the text. You don't have to write complete sentences.

1 What two historical facts about the didgeridoo are there in the text? *(2 things)*

____

____

2 What are didgeridoos made from?

____

3 When a didgeridoo is made, what's the most difficult part?

____

____

____

4 What two kinds of didgeridoo does the text warn you about? *(2 things)*

____

____

5 If a tourist who wants to learn to play the didgeridoo follows the tourist office's advice, what should he or she do?

____

____

LANGUAGE

___/22

1 WORDS Who or what is it?

___/7

Explain the meaning of the following words or expressions from Unit 1, Part A and B in your own words.

Paraphrasing **(etwas mit anderen Worten erklären)**
- **Umschreibe** das Wort, das du beschreiben möchtest mit einem anderen Wort: *'to wonder' is the same as 'to ask yourself'*
- **Nenne das Gegenteil:** *'alive' is the opposite of 'dead'*
- Finde ein **allgemeines Wort** und nenne **Eigenschaften**: *racing car = a very fast car*
- Umschreibe mit ... **is/are like** ...: *A chef **is like** a cook.*
- Verwende einen **Relativsatz**: *A garage **is a place where** ...; a nurse **is a person who** ...*
- Diese Übung passt zum Skills File *Paraphrasing* auf S. 148 in deinem Englischbuch.

1 orphan

The children have without parents.

2 ancestor

My ancestor is my mother and my father

3 (to) wash the dishes

wash the plate

4 (to) apologize

I hur a person.

5 (to) recommend

The movie was good and I tell a person

6 (to) introduce sb.

I show my new friend my mother

7 (to) repeat

I pratice my vacuble that is repeat.

2 GRAMMAR Ron was on the radio

_____/7

Indirekte Rede

- Wenn das einleitende Verb in der Vergangenheit steht *(simple past)*, werden die Zeiten in der indirekten Rede um eine Zeitstufe verschoben.
  Sue says, 'He's 15 years old.' ▶ *Sue said he was 15 years old.*
- Dies sind die wichtigen Veränderungen:
  present (she is) ▶ *past (she was)*
  past (she was) ▶ *past perfect (she had been)*
  can (she can be) ▶ *could (she could be)*
  will-future (she will be) ▶ *would + infinitive (she would be)*
  going to-future (she is going to be) ▶ *was/were going to + infinitive (she was going to be)*
  present perfect (she has been) ▶ *past perfect (she had been)*
- Zu dieser Übung passt das Grammar File 4 auf S. 163 in deinem Englischbuch.

Last week there was a programme on the radio about sports. This is what Ron said on the radio.

I'm 16 years old and I live near Perth together with my family. I love sports. I'm in the Australian football team. I don't play every week because I don't have much time. I want to play at least twice a month in the future.

Sue couldn't listen to the programme so Alison reports what Ron said. Complete the text. Use ***indirect speech****.*

Ron said that he ____________________ 16 years old and ____________________ near Perth together with his family. He said that he ____________________ sports and that he ____________________ in the Australian football team. He said that he ____________________ every week because he ____________________ much time. He said that he ____________________ to play at least twice a month in the future.

3 GRAMMAR Jill left a note

____/8

*Jill's father found Jill's note when he got home from work. Later her mother calls him and asks questions about Jill. Answer her questions. Use **indirect speech**. Be careful with the tenses.*

> Hi Mum, hi Dad,
> I'm at Jane's house. I won't be home for tea. We're still working on our presentation for school because we haven't finished it yet. But I think it'll be really good. We're going to present it to you on Tuesday evening. I'll be back by 8 o'clock.
> Jill

Mum Hello Matt, is Jill at home?

Dad No, she isn't. But I found a note. It said that ______________________________

____

____

____

____

____ on Tuesday evening.

Mum Oh yes, I remember. When will she be back? Did the note say anything?

Dad Yes, it did. The note said ______________________________

____

Mum That's OK. Thanks and see you later. Bye.

Dad Yes, bye.

WRITING

____ /15

A surfing accident

Joe, Jim and Ann from Canberra spent two weeks at the coast near Sydney. First they took surfing lessons and one day they went surfing on their own.

Look at the pictures and write an exciting story about what happened. Write 120–150 words in your exercise book.

- Benutze beim Verfassen deiner Geschichte **linking words** *(because, but, that, who, after some time, suddenly, then, next ...)*, **beschreibende Adjektive** *(the young boy)* und **Adverbien** *(..., she added nervously)*.
- Schreibe die Geschichte im **simple past**.
- Lies deine Geschichte am Ende noch einmal durch und **korrigiere** deinen Text.
- Weitere Tipps findest du im Skills File auf S. 150–51 in deinem Englischbuch.

Start like this:

Last Monday Joe, Jim and Ann, three close friends from Canberra, went surfing near Sydney. When they arrived at the beach, they got changed quickly and went into the water ...

SPEAKING

____/15

I can tell you more

a) *Find yourself a partner and act out the role play together.*

Imagine you're staying at a campsite in the south of France. You meet the British boy/girl who is staying in the caravan next to yours for the first time.

Start your conversation politely and introduce yourselves. Ask and answer questions. Ask for help or give help if you need to. End your conversation in a friendly way. Take ten minutes to prepare your dialogue.

Partner A: the German boy/girl

- you arrived the evening before
- you're from Saarbrücken
- you go camping every year
- this is your first time at this campsite
- you want to find out more about the campsite (pool? / disco? / café? / how far to the beach?)
- you're interested in swimming in the sea

Partner B: the British boy/girl

- you arrived 10 days ago
- you're from Glasgow, Scotland
- you love camping
- it's the third time you've been to the campsite, weather always great
- you know a lot (pool ► near the reception / café on campsite, opposite supermarket / disco ► outside the campsite once a week on Friday / beach ► five minutes' walk
- you want to go to the beach in half an hour

b) *Swap roles and have a second go. This time, you both really hate camping and the weather is awful.*

Partner A: the German boy/girl

- you arrived the evening before
- you're from Chemnitz
- you go camping every year, at this campsite for the first time
- you hate camping
- you'd like a holiday in a hotel more
- you like going to the beach (say why!)
- end the conversation

Partner B: the British boy/girl

- you arrived 10 days ago
- you're from Cardiff, Wales
- this is your third time at this campsite, this year weather bad: rain, cold ...
- you hate camping
- you'd like a holiday in a hotel more (say why!)
- you want to get to know European cities and go somewhere different every year
- use your own ideas to end the the conversation

Gesamtpunktzahl ______ / 64 Note ______

READING

____ / 15

Seventeen Plus

Tony's job and career corner

Dear readers,

Every week I get a lot of e-mails from young people who are having trouble deciding what to do when they finish school. I often hear questions like "How can I find the job that suits me best?" or "How can I decide at my age what I want to do for the rest of my life?" So, in order to help you out, I talked to some young people who were in this difficult situation one or two years ago. I'm sure you'll find what they have to say useful. Good luck!

Tony

When I found myself in year ten, I suddenly noticed that I didn't have any real plans for my future. I knew that for a lot of jobs you need experience before you can start – that's why I volunteered to help at our local zoo. I worked there twice a week for three hours in the afternoon – believe me, it wasn't always easy! Anyway, I enjoyed working with the animals and after a few weeks the zookeepers let me work on my own. They liked the way I worked and felt comfortable giving me the opportunity to work independently. Working with the animals helped me to become more confident. Some months later the zoo was looking for an apprentice zookeeper. A lot of people were interested in the position – there were 24 applications including mine. I was chosen for the position mainly because of my work experience. So far the apprenticeship has been going really well! Paul, 17, Chester

I love art and throughout year 10 I kept asking myself, "How can you make money with art?" I mean, money isn't the most important thing in a job. I think it's important to do a job which you like, but of course you need money for everyday life. I was lucky to get a part-time summer job at the Museum for Modern Art after I had finished school. Not an amazing job, but after spending years in the classroom I enjoyed working – no matter what I had to do! Then I found out that the museum also did educational projects with young children. My part-time job left me enough free time so I took part in the kids' arts workshops at the museum whenever I could. I liked it so much that I applied for work experience with the education team. I did that for half a year and was lucky because I could still live with my parents. So I didn't have to pay for a flat. After that I decided to go on to art college, where I am now. I hope to find a job working with kids in a museum later. Work experience really opened my eyes to what I want from life. Nora, 19, York

I think any kind of work experience is a good thing, but it took me quite a long time to get used to the idea of working for no money. Still, you learn a lot about teamwork, communication and relationships. Many companies look for people with work experience, so don't forget to add any work experience you have to your CV. If possible, enclose any feedback you got so that companies get to know what qualifications and skills you have. And one last thing – sometimes work experience just helps you to find out what you don't want to do in your future life – even then it's a good thing. Lea, 20, Exeter

→

Who says what?

a) *Read the text and write Tony (1x), Paul (3x), Nora (2x) or Lea (4x) at the beginning of each sentence. (10P)*

________________ thinks that work experience makes you more confident.

________________ wants to help young people look for a job.

________________ thinks it's important to like your job.

________________ says that finding a job is easier if you've already done some work experience.

________________ didn't know what he wanted to do after school.

________________ says it's good to hand in any references you have.

________________ thinks that work experience can help you decide what subject you want to study.

________________ applied for a position along with a lot of other people.

________________ thought that work experience should be paid.

________________ says you should tell companies about your work experience when you apply.

b) *Look at the text again and answer the following questions in three to five words.*
You don't have to write complete sentences. (5P)

1 What was the relationship between the zookeepers and Paul like?

____

2 Why did Nora have enough time to take part in the kids' courses?

____

3 In Lea's opinion, what are the advantages and disadvantages of work experience? *(three things)*

____

____

____

____

LANGUAGE

____/24

1 WORDS Your jobs mind map

____/17

a) *Make a mind map for the topic "jobs". Use the new vocabulary from unit 2. The numbers tell you how many words you should be able to add to each word group. You can add more words as you work through the unit. (13P)*

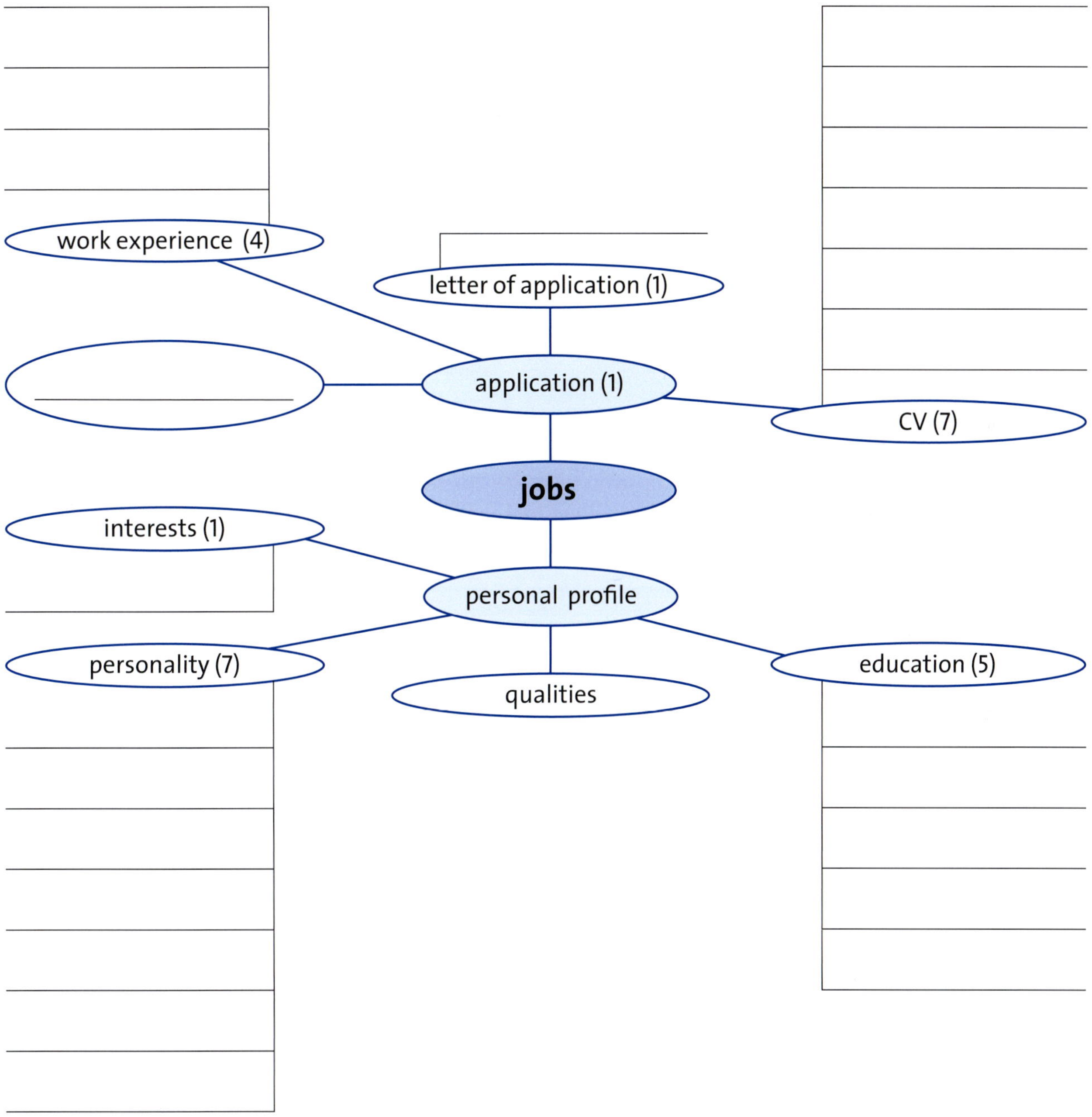

b) *Choose **four** nouns from your mind map and write sentences for each one. (4P)*

2 GRAMMAR Paul's interview at the zoo

____/7

When Paul went for his interview at the zoo, this is what he said to the manager:

2 I can start the apprenticeship as soon as you want.

3 I like working with your animals very much.

4 I get on well with the other zookeepers.

1 I've been working at the zoo for a few months now.

5 I will work hard if I get the apprenticeship.

After the interview at the zoo, the manager told a second zookeeper what Paul had said.
Write what the manager said.

Indirekte Rede
- Beachte die Veränderungen der Zeitformen in der **indirekten Rede**! Eine Übersicht findest du im Grammar File 4 auf Seite 163 in deinem Englischbuch.
- Wenn du noch unsicher bist, notiere dir zunächst die Zeitform in der direkten Rede und schreibe sie hinter die Sätze in direkter Rede. Nach einem Pfeil ergänzt du dann die erforderliche Zeitform in der indirekten Rede:
  *I **saw** many animals. – simple past ▸ past perfect*

WRITING

____/15

Sue Evans lives in Bristol. She has seen this advert and wants to apply for the job. Write her application letter. Write something about her skills and why she would be good for this job.

Förmliche Briefe *(formal letters)*
Wichtige Punkte:
- Adresse ohne Namen
- vollständige Anschrift
- Datum
- höfliche Anrede
- Langformen verwenden
- Brief in Absätze gliedern
- Ende: Dank im Voraus, höfliche Schlussformel, Unterschrift, getippter Name

Einen Beispielbrief findest du im Skills File auf S. 153 in deinem Englischbuch.

The Bristol Times 2 November 2011

St. John's Residential Care Home

We are looking for a **young volunteer** (m/f) to teach a small group (12 people) basic computer skills, including using the internet and writing e-mails. The classes will take place once a week for one hour.

At St. John's we have 80 residents and consider it extremely important to offer a wide range of free-time activities.

Are you interested in working with people and sharing your IT skills? We would provide training after Christmas. Please tell us which days of the week would suit you best.

Sorry, we can't pay anything but we will be happy to give you a reference.

Please send your application letter plus CV to:

Ms Alice Spring
St. John's Residential Care Home
4 New Garden Street
Bristol BS1 3AD

STUDY SKILLS

____/10

Look at the advertisement from St. John's Residential Care Home again. Now imagine you want to apply. Write your CV.

Sieh dir das Beispiel für einen Lebenslauf in deinem Englischbuch auf S. 39 oder im Skills File auf S. 152 noch einmal an, bevor du mit dem Schreiben deines Lebenslaufs beginnst.

Klassenarbeit B

Gesamtpunktzahl ohne Speaking	____ / 94	Note ____
Gesamtpunktzahl mit Speaking	____ / 122	Note ____

LISTENING

____ / 22

Are you happy with your job?

The radio programme Radio Today has a themed week on the topic 'Are you happy with your job?' Each morning between ten and eleven another person is interviewed.

04 1 Terry and Alice

____ / 11

a) *Listen to the interview.*

When Alice left school, she was 17 and didn't know at all which job she should choose.
The pictures show Alice's career. Put them in the right order. There is one more picture than you need. (5P)

A

B

C

D

E

F

b) *Read the task. Then listen to the interview again and tick if the statements are true or false. (6P)*

	True	False
1 Alice had always wanted to work in a TV shop.		
2 Alice moved out of her parents' home because she had problems with her parents.		
3 When Alice worked in the supermarket, she tried to find out her strengths.		
4 Alice wants to be a millionaire one day.		
5 Alice does not go on holidays very often.		
6 Alice is still looking for a fulfilling job.		

2 Terry and Harry

____/11

05 ***a)*** *Terry's next guest Harry has just written a book.*

Read the task. Then listen to the radio show ***until the break*** *and answer the questions in one to seven words or numbers. (6P)*

1 How did Harry find out that he did a good job as a careers advisor?

____

2 Why did he decide to work part-time?

____

3 What was the most important step in his career?

____

4 How can you describe what Harry's book is about?

____

5 What makes the book so interesting?

____

6 Why is Harry happy in his job?

____

Harry (28) is an expert on jobs.

b) *After the break, Harry and Terry talk a bit more about the book. Read the task. Then listen to the dialogue and match the beginnings and endings of the sentences. There is one more ending than you need. (5P)*

1 When you're looking for a job take time and ...	A match your interests with different jobs.
2 The game in the book helps you to ...	B practise them very often.
3 A good help with job interviews is to ...	C find out what you're good at.
4 If you don't get a job, you shouldn't ...	D work for your parents or family.
5 Not in every good job you will ...	E worry.
	F earn much money.

LANGUAGE

_____ / 40

1 WORDS Getting by in English

_____ / 5

Sage, dass ...

1 ... die Lehrerin erwartet, dass ihr eure Hausaufgaben macht.

____

2 ... sich bis heute erst fünf Schüler freiwillig gemeldet haben.

____

3 ... es dir nichts ausmacht, neben dem Fenster zu sitzen.

____

4 ... du zehn Minuten gewartet hast, bevor dich die Verkäuferin bedient hat.

____

5 ... du entschlossen bist, nicht anzufangen zu rauchen.

____

2 WORDS Different jobs

____ / 8

a) Read the job descriptions and fill in the correct words. (4P)

1 Somebody who works in a kindergarten is a ______________________.

2 Somebody who cooks in a restaurant is a ______________________.

3 Somebody who often helps people who want to lose weight by doing more sport is a

______________________.

4 Somebody who repairs cars is a ______________________.

b) Explain in English what these people do. (4P)

In Unit 1 auf S.16 findest du mehr Hilfen zum Thema *Paraphrasing*.

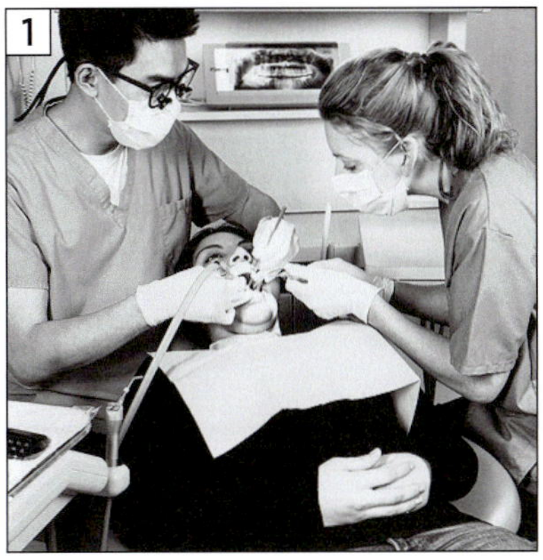

1 *A dentist's assistant* ______________________

____

2 ______________________

____

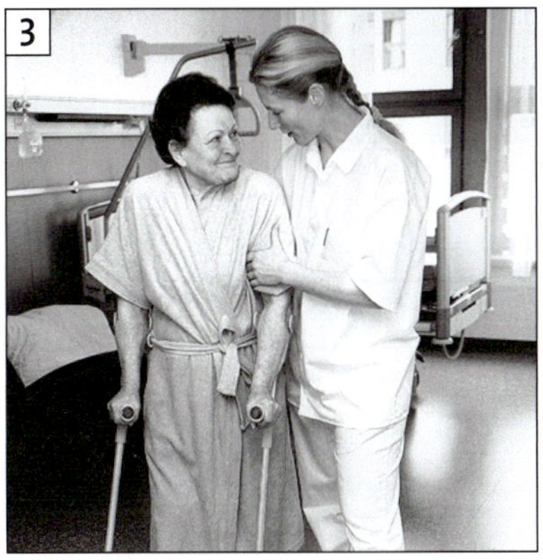

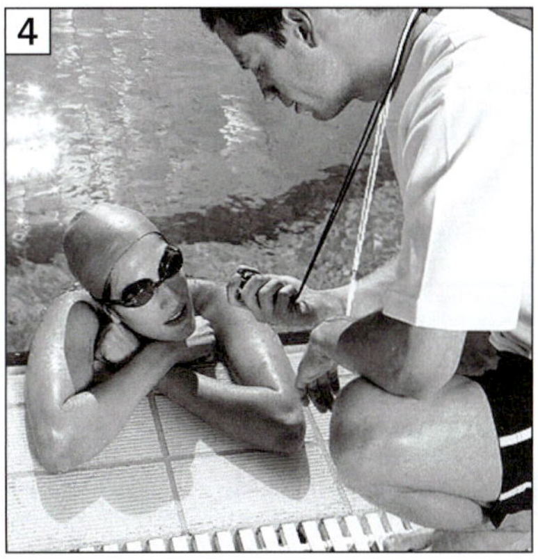

3 ______________________

____

4 ______________________

____

3 WORDS Just look at my letter!

____ / 8

Complete the text with words from the box. Be careful: There are three more words than you need. Make sure you use the correct form of the nouns.

(to) apply for • apprenticeship • candidate • (to) impress • interview • necessary • qualification • suitable • tie • (to) vote • weakness

I'm so happy! I just got an invitation for a job ____________________. It's for an ____________________ in a hotel. I think there'll be quite a few ____________________ though so I must try ____________________ the manager. I'm going to work out what I want to say during the interview. I know that I'll have to talk about myself, about my ____________________ but also about my ____________________. And I'll have to think of some questions to ask! Oh, I also need to go to the shops to look for some ____________________ clothes and I'm going to wear a ____________________.

4 GRAMMAR Parents!

____ / 6

*Your parents give you lots of advice because they want you to get good marks in your exams. You tell a friend about their advice. Write the sentences in **indirect speech** in your exercise book.*

1 Do your homework every day.
2 Don't talk during lessons.
3 Please get up earlier in the morning.

4 Please have a good breakfast every day.
5 Don't stay out too long at night.
6 Study with your friends in the afternoon.

5 GRAMMAR Information for my teacher

___/5

*You have been asked to find out about different jobs for school, so you have interviewed a group of people. Your teacher wants to know the questions you asked. Use **indirect speech**.*

1 What do you do on a normal day at work?
2 At what age did you decide on your career?
3 What do you like most about your job?
4 What will your next career steps be?
5 Have you ever thought about doing another job?

Start like this:

1 I asked them what they ___

2 ___

3 ___

4 ___

5 ___

6 GRAMMAR A talk with the neighbour

___/8

*You talked to your neighbour about his job. The next day you tell your friend about it. Complete the sentences with the correct verb and the correct form in **indirect speech**.*

☞ Du kannst diese Übung in zwei Schritten lösen:
1. Was sagen die beiden Person in der **direkten Rede**? Welche Zeitform ist erforderlich?
2. Wende dann die Regeln für die Rückverschiebung der Zeitformen in der **indirekten Rede** an. (Grammar File 4 auf S. 163 in deinem Englischbuch)

(to) be (2x) • (to) come (2x) • (to) have • (to) need • (to) work (2x)

I told our neighbour that I ___ doing a project for school about jobs and that I was interested in talking to a builder about his work. He said that he ___ for a big building company in Liverpool. He added that he ___ his job for over twenty years now. He said that he and the other workers ___ outside all day.

I told him that I ___ the information for a presentation. He thought that it ___ a good thing to learn about jobs at school. He also said that I ___ to see one of the houses he was building at the moment. I said that I ___ the following week.

MEDIATION

____ / 17

Talking about an advert

There is an international school near your home in Germany which is looking for a childcare assistant. You have seen their advert in the newspaper and want to apply. Your mother doesn't understand everything so you need to explain the advert to her. Read the advert, then answer your mum's questions in German.

International School South West

is looking for a

part-time after-school childcare assistant

Monday to Friday during the school year from 16:15 to 17:15
Starting next February

Your role:

- looking after 1st grade children
- supporting our professional childcare assistants
- playing with children indoors and outdoors

Applicants should:

- have experience working with children
- be reliable and flexible
- be sporty
- be able to work with children, parents and teachers
- have very good English (second language) communication skills, written and oral
- speak at least one other foreign language

Please send your electronic application letter in English (plus references) to

Mr Adam Pauls
Director
application@issw.de

Deine Mutter Also jetzt gehen wir die Anzeige noch mal zusammen durch, ich habe nämlich nicht alles so genau verstanden. Was für eine Stelle ist genau ausgeschrieben? *(mindestens drei Dinge)*

Du ______________________________

____

____

Deine Mutter Und was musst du da genau machen? *(drei Dinge)*

Du ______________________________

____

____

Deine Mutter Das klingt ja ganz gut. Aber musst du da keine Erzieherausbildung haben?

Du ______________________________

____

Deine Mutter Und welche persönlichen Eigenschaften muss ein Bewerber mitbringen? *(vier Dinge)*

Du ______________________________

____

____

Deine Mutter Wie sieht es denn mit den Fremdsprachenkenntnissen aus? *(drei Dinge)*

Du ______________________________

____

____

____

Deine Mutter Ich glaube, du könntest dich da bewerben. Ruf doch gleich mal an.

Du ______________________________

____

Deine Mutter Und was musst du da noch beachten? *(zwei Dinge)*

Du ______________________________

____

WRITING

____ / 15

A person who loves her job

Think of people you know who are really happy with their job. Choose one of your parents, a brother or sister, your uncle, your neighbour or an imaginary person. Write about 120 words.

Write about ...
- who the person is,
- what kind of job they do,
- their role in their job – what they have to do
- their qualifications
- their working hours and
- why you think this person is happy with their job.

Finish your text with your opinion about the job.

SPEAKING

____/28

06 A job interview

Josh has applied for an apprenticeship as a mechanic in a garage. Listen to Josh's interview with Mr Preston, the manager of the garage.

07 Now you

Now it is your turn to do a job interview. Imagine you have applied for an apprenticeship.

There are some ideas for jobs in the box below. Choose one job or use your own ideas. Then listen to the questions on the CD and practice your interview.

a vet's assistant • an IT assistant • a customer adviser in a big department store or at a travel agent's • a make up artist at the theatre • a bank clerk • a cook • a nurse

Ein *job interview* üben

- Wenn du einen Beruf ausgewählt hast, kannst du dir Notizen machen: Warum möchtest du diesen Beruf erlernen, welche besonderen Fähigkeiten hast du und welche Fragen möchtest du am Ende stellen?
- Natürlich kannst du das Interview auch mit einem Partner durchführen. Dadurch wird das Interview noch realistischer, weil dein Interviewpartner genau auf deine Äußerungen eingehen kann. Hört euch dazu das Interview gemeinsam an. Dein Interviewpartner kann sich Fragen notieren oder die Fragen aus dem Lösungsheft vorlesen.

Klassenarbeit A

Gesamtpunktzahl ohne Speaking	______ / 58	Note	______
Gesamtpunktzahl mit Speaking	______ / 72	Note	______

LISTENING

______ / 21

A presentation about graffiti

A group of three students is giving a presentation about graffiti. Now it's Paul's turn to talk about 'What graffiti can mean to people'. In preparation for his presentation, he has done some interviews. Listen to his interview partners.

08 ***a)*** *Paul and the policeman*

Read the task and listen to what the policeman thought about graffiti. Mark a), b), c) or d). (3P)

1 The policeman says that graffiti can be found ...	a) mostly on people's houses.	
	b) everywhere in the city but mostly in underground stations.	
	c) on houses, buildings, trains and in underground stations.	
	d) on official buildings and in underground stations.	
2 For policemen like him graffiti means ...	a) a lot of phone calls.	
	b) a lot of cleaning.	
	c) a waste of money.	
	d) a lot of time spent travelling round the city.	
3 One of his ideas for fighting graffiti is that ...	a) every sprayer should get an ASBO.	
	b) a special paint should be put on buildings to protect them from sprayers.	
	c) sprayers should help to clean the graffiti off walls.	
	d) there should be special walls for sprayers.	

09 ***b)*** *The art teacher*

Read the task. While listening to the art teacher's opinion, fill in the missing information.
You do not have to write complete sentences. (8P)

1 What is her school project about? *(three facts)*

____

____

____

____

2 Where shouldn't graffiti be sprayed? *(two facts)*

____

3 When is graffiti art? *(two facts)*

____

____

4 What is her opinion on the future of graffiti?

____

____

10 ***c)*** *The girl and Paul's conclusion*

Read the task. While listening to the girl and to Paul's conclusion, complete the sentences. (10P)

1 She would like to do graffiti ______________________.

2 She practises graffiti ______________________ and ______________________.

3 Through her graffiti she wants to show people how ______________________.

4 There is a German artist who does graffiti on the walls of a ______________________.

5 She hopes to become ______________________.

6 In her opinion, graffiti makes places ______________________.

7 She thinks ______________________.

8 Paul concludes that some people ______________________,

but others ______________________.

LANGUAGE

____ / 27

1 WORDS New graffiti at the station

____ / 5

On her way to work, Mary sees some new graffiti on one of the station walls. Complete the sentences with the correct words.

Adjektive
Mache dir vor der Bearbeitung der Aufgabe nochmals die Bedeutung der jeweiligen beiden Wörter klar,
z. B. **surprised** = überrasch**t**, aber **surprising** = überrasch**end**
interested = interessier**t**, aber **interesting** = interess**ant**

1 I was ______________________ (surprised/surprising) when I passed the station the other day. What had happened? Someone had graffitied one of the walls.

2 I was very impressed by the graffiti, but it was ______________________ (surprise/surprising) how many people didn't seem to notice the new graffiti as they walked past.

3 Weren't they ______________________ (interested/interesting) in graffiti? Or were they just in a hurry so that they didn't see anything at all?

4 It's ______________________ (depressed/depressing) that people don't notice what is around them.

5 I really like graffiti but I'm a bit ______________________ (worried/worrying) about the person who sprayed it. If the police catch them, they will have to pay a lot of money and get an ASBO.

2 WORDS John talks about what happened yesterday morning

____ / 7

Complete the sentences with words from the box. Be careful: there are three more words than you need. Use the correct form of the verbs.

as usual • busy • finally • (to) give sth up • (to) go by • (to) miss • perhaps • public • secretly • (to) set the alarm clock

I always ______________________ for 7 o'clock. When the alarm clock rang yesterday, I turned it off ______________________ and then I fell asleep again because I was still very tired. Time ______________________ quickly and when I ______________________ woke up again it was 7.50! Oh dear – what was I going to do? I had hoped that my mum would give me a lift to school but she was already ______________________ in her office. So I ran to the bus stop, but of course I ______________________ the bus. I ran home again to get my bike. ______________________ I would still make it to school on time.

3 WORDS Using new words

___/5

*Here are some more new words from Unit 3. Choose **five** of them and write sentences for each one.*

worrying • (to) punish • (to) behave • wedding • receipt • (to) save • (to) be addicted to sth.

____

____

____

____

____

4 GRAMMAR Graffiti in a church

___/10

Understanding participle clauses
Dieses Thema ist in deinem Englischbuch als **additional information** gekennzeichnet.
Bereite es für die Klassenarbeit vor, wenn ihr **participle clauses** im Unterricht behandelt habt.

*Read this short newspaper article by Alan Smith, a reporter for a British newspaper in Germany. Then work on **a)** and **b)**.*

a) *Which sentences contain a participle clause? Underline the participle forms. (5P)*

A Catholic[1] church in the south of Germany, built in 1961, has got a new look thanks to a local graffiti artist.
The church in Kehl, near the Black Forest, agreed to the project after a long public discussion.
When the idea was first suggested, many people living in the quiet town were against the project. However, a group who supported the artist, Stefan Strumbel, invited everybody to an open discussion about the project. When he presented his ideas for the new-look church, which included a large graffiti showing Mary with the baby Jesus above the entrance, Strumbel was able to win over the town. His ideas became very popular.
"I'm open to modern art," said one man. "But graffiti in a church? That was new to me. But look here: the empty speech bubbles sprayed on this wall have already been filled in with prayers and wishes. This shows us that people visiting our church are getting involved."

b) *Translate the sentences with participle forms into German. Write the sentences in your exercise book. (5P)*

[1] Catholic ['kæθlɪk] *katholisch*

MEDIATION

____ / 10

A voucher for an audio book

Deine Mutter möchte ihr Englisch verbessern. Sie hat diesen Gutschein für Hörbücher erhalten und bittet dich, ihr zu helfen, weil sie nicht alles genau versteht.

Erkläre ...
- um was für einen Gutschein es sich handelt.
- wie man vorgehen muss *(fünf Dinge)*.
- was kostenlos ist.
- unter welchen Umständen man bezahlen muss, wofür man wie viel bezahlen muss und ob man auf jeden Fall bezahlen muss.

Aufgaben zur Mediation lösen
Bei dieser Aufgabe kommt es nicht darauf an, wortwörtlich ins Deutsch zu übersetzen. Lies den Text genau und übertrage dann das Wesentliche sinngemäß ins Deutsche.

Download three free audio books ... and listen to all your favourite books whenever, wherever you want!

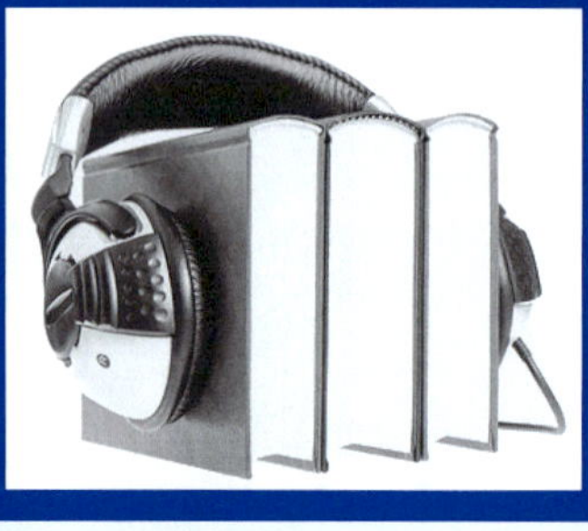

1. Visit www.yourfreeaudiobook.com/voucher
2. Create your account.
3. Choose your audio books from over 20,000 books in our collection.
4. Download and save them to listen to wherever you go.

After your free 20 days, you'll become a member automatically. You'll receive one audio book for £8.99 per month.
If you decide not to be a member of yourfreeaudiobook before the end of your free 20 days, you don't have to pay anything.

See www.yourfreeaudiobook.com for more information.

SPEAKING

____/14

11 A school trip

Sandra and Adam are discussing their school trip. Listen to their conversation.

Having a discussion
- Mache dir während des Hörens Notizen zu Redewendungen, die du in Diskussionen verwenden kannst. Unterscheide zwischen Ausdrücken zur Meinungsäußerung, Argumenten und Beispielen sowie Zustimmung, Ablehnung und Nachfragen zum Verständnis.
- Lies dazu auch das Skills File auf S.147 in deinem Englischbuch.

Now you

Your class wants to go on a school trip. There are two possibilities: you could go either to Berlin or to London. Have a discussion about the trip with your English classmate. You start the discussion.

For this discussion you should find yourself a partner. One of you should be for Berlin, one for London.

Before you start, collect some arguments for or against the two cities. There are already some notes in the table. Use these ideas or add some more.

	Journey	How long?	Where to stay	Costs	Free time	Sightseeing	Evening programme	...
Berlin	by train	five days	hostel city centre	€250 + pocket money		learn about German history		
London	by plane	four days	families outside London	€340 + pocket money	get to know about the British way of life		stay at home with families	

Klassenarbeit B

Gesamtpunktzahl ______ / 79 Note ______

READING

______ / 19

The new youth club

After three long years, the youth club was reopened last Friday. At the opening party Mayor Daniel Cooper talked about the past, the present and the future of the youth club. He said that problems with vandalism, drugs and alcohol had led to the closing of the youth club three years ago. "Knowing that a youth club plays an important role in a town like ours, we started working on a new concept right away," said Mayor Daniel Cooper.

And he went on "I'm happy that we were able to work together with Steve Miller, who is now the leader of our youth club. Being a social worker, he succeeded in involving young people right from the start. His ideas and the way he went up to people and talked to them were the key to working out a successful concept for our new youth club."

At the party Sarah, 16, told us, "there was a group of 15 young people in the planning team. Before we started working on 'our favourite concept' for our youth club, we visited quite a few youth clubs in our area and talked to people there. We then collected ideas for all sorts of activities we wanted to have in our youth club. Knowing about the activities was important for planning it. A lot of time went by before we could actually start planning the building. But this surely was the most interesting part of our work."

"It was the two architects' job to listen very carefully to our young people's wishes and their ideas before they set out to plan the building. And, as you can see today, they did a really good job. Thanks to many local companies who sponsored this project with a lot of money we were able to build this fabulous building," Daniel Cooper proudly told us.

"We have taken the first step." added Steve Miller the social worker. "Now we want to involve as many young people as possible. Surveys show that children who belong to youth clubs are more confident and will not have so many problems with drugs and alcohol. In many cities young people just go to the club when they feel like it, but in our club young people are asked to take an active part and work together in teams. They can be the leader of one of the groups for younger kids or even become a member of the youth club team which runs the club and discusses new ideas for the club together with the social workers and myself."

Sarah talked about the activities: "We offer all kinds of activities from football to drama groups and even help with the homework. Of course there are six computers with internet access, printer and scanner. Many of the activities are only possible with the help of young volunteers. This is part of the concept. Now a name has to be found." "We didn't want to look for a name before the youth club has opened. I'm sure it will be easy to agree on a good name once we have worked together for a few weeks," said Steve Miller.

D5 Erweiterte Ausgabe

English G 21

Klassenarbeitstrainer

für Schülerinnen und Schüler

Lösungen und Lerntipps

Cornelsen

LISTENING

01 1 A high school photo competition

(...)

Mrs Miller	You each have your cards in front of you. For a start, I'd just like to start; my personal favourite is number three.
Mr Bush	You're kidding!
Lesley	Really?
Mrs Miller	Yeah.
Mr Bush	Number three?
Mrs Miller	Yeah, I find this use of contrast fantastic, I think the colours are beautiful, a beautiful lonely pier, stretching out to the horizon. You could almost be walking along it.
Mr Bush	I mean I guess you could, could imagine yourself sitting on the edge of the wharf, putting your legs in the water, but for me it's not really Australia.
Lesley	Australia, exactly, that's what I was thinking.
Mr Bush	You think the same?
Lesley	It's not really Australia because, well it is Australia, but it's not, it doesn't say Australia to me.
Mr Bush	It could be anywhere.
Lesley	Exactly, it could be like the Caribbean or ...
Mrs Miller	It could be anywhere, it could be anywhere but we don't want to necessarily fall into these clichés as well.
Mr Bush	What about number five, the sailing boat? I mean that's, that's ...
Lesley	Oh you like it 'cause you're a sailor, Mr Bush.
Mrs Miller	Yeah you like sailing Mr Bush.
Mr Bush	OK, OK, but I mean it's a brilliant image, I mean.
Lesley	It is a great image but once again that could be, I don't know, in Spain or something, I mean I know we don't want to go cliché Australia but ...
Mr Bush	OK, OK.
Mrs Miller	The colours certainly are beautiful in that picture ... the blue is fabulous ...
Mr Bush	Number two is for me a bit like a postcard really.
Lesley	Yeah, I agree.
Mr Bush	I mean, just look at those rocks, the way they just jut out of the sea, it's fantastic, it's a great image. But, the thing is, the rocks, and the beach ...this is the Twelve Apostles, it's like a postcard photo. I mean, I know that place, it looks like that ...
Mrs Miller	Number two, I mean how many times have we seen that photo before?
Lesley	Yeah that's true.
Mr Bush	And, what about number one Lesley, what do you think of that?
Lesley	I like number one and number six.
Mrs Miller	I like number one too.
Lesley	Yeah?

Mrs Miller I like number one, this new view of, of the skyline at night, I was, yeah it's beautiful.

Mr Bush Is that from the North shore do you think?

Lesley No, I think that's from the Eastern shore because the Harbour Bridge is on the right, but I want to talk about number six if I can because, I mean, that for me is such a brilliant shot because you can see faintly in the background the Sydney Harbour Bridge and then in the foreground is all this movement.

Mrs Miller You're right and, you just, it's the simplicity of children playing is really nice, isn't it?

Lesley Yeah, so fun, peacefulness, summer.

Mrs Miller Also it's not cliché; we haven't seen that picture before.

Lesley Exactly! Yeah, I don't know, I, I really like number six, six or one for me.

Mr Bush Well, I'd say one is out of it but number, number four is for me a typical, um, look at that white sand, and the foliage, the green leaves ...

Lesley Yeah, but there's no movement in it. Do you know what I mean?

Mr Bush The clouds, the clouds ...

Lesley So what do you think? Number six?

Mr Bush Well, I mean ...

Lesley Number six, number six ...

Mr Bush You're speaking from the students' viewpoint, so ...

Mrs Miller I'm personally torn between number six, number three and number one.

Lesley OK, and I like number six, so that's two for number six ...

Mr Bush Alright, alright, alright, two to one ... Anyway, I can see what you're saying about number six, it's just, you know, it's just this darkness underneath is a little bit ... anyway, but I could live with number six.

Lesley Yeah? Great. – Number six?

Mrs Miller Yeah, good.

Mr Bush So, when will you tell the kids?

Mrs Miller Well, I'll let the kids know in assembly tomorrow. (...)

a)

A2, B3, C6, D1, E4, F5

b)

1b), 2c), 3a), 4c), 5c), 6a)

02 2 An interview for the school radio station

Steve Hello there fellow students, teachers and anyone else who's listening, this is Steve broadcasting live from Caroline Chisholm High's radio station, and in the studio with me today we have Maya. Hello Maya!

Maya Hi Steve!

Steve Um, Maya is this year's winner of the photo competition. Congratulations!

Maya Thank you.

Steve So how old are you, Maya?

Maya I'm 16, I'm in year 9.

Steve Year 9? OK, and, um, is this the first time that you've participated in a competition?

Maya No, no, I was in it, um, a couple of years ago. I didn't get anywhere the other time so this is the second time, yep.

Steve OK, and what was the photograph you took a couple of years ago?

Maya Erm, I think it was something of my family, yeah.

Steve Oh really?

Maya Yeah.

Steve So you've been taking photos for quite some time?

Maya Yeah, I started ten years ago when I was six ...

Steve Wow!

Maya Yeah, I got a camera for my birthday and, um, and yeah I started on my birthday.

Steve Yeah wow.

Maya So I just started taking photos and yeah ...

Steve And you haven't stopped since.

Maya Not really no.

Steve Wow, so, um, tell us, the photo that you took, um, tell us a little bit about the photo or what inspired you to take it.

Maya Well, like I said, the other time I was in the competition I took a photograph of my family, and so I've always, I've never really liked like touristy shots, it's like it's not really, they're not my best photographs ...

Steve Sure.

Maya My best photographs are always the things like, photographs of my family, people that I knew really well that I could get closer to and so this time I just walked around a lot in my neighbourhood and looked at places that I knew really well and, um, and yeah, and so ...

Steve And, and this was it?

Maya Yeah, I just got lucky with the light I think and yeah ...

Steve Excellent, um, just for the people who maybe haven't seen the photograph do you wanna explain a little bit about the, where you were, or kind of the context of the photograph?

Maya Well, yeah there's a park and it's really open, green space, um, and it looks out over the harbour, you can see the Harbour Bridge in the distance, but there's a, in the centreground of the photograph there's a kids' playground and there's a slide going down one direction and swings on the other one and somebody's swinging right the way back ... um, so that it's kind of opposite direction from the slide so there's a contrast and the sun's setting behind it so ...

→

Steve Yeah, and for those of you who haven't seen it, it really is a splendid and beautiful photo. Um, so tell me how did you feel when the art teacher announced that you were this year's winner?

Maya Oh my god, I was so excited! I was just like, oh my god! 'cause I didn't get anywhere the other time and I was like "wow" and my friends were like "cool, yeah, good one!", you know so ...

Steve Excellent, excellent ... And for those of us who don't know, can you tell us what the prize is?

Maya Um, it's a really good camera, high quality camera, much better than the one I've got, the pixel rate is really good and yeah really good lens, so I'm looking forward to trying it out!

Steve Wow, excellent, alright, well thanks a lot Maya, and thanks a lot everybody else for joining us! See you soon.

Maya Bye!

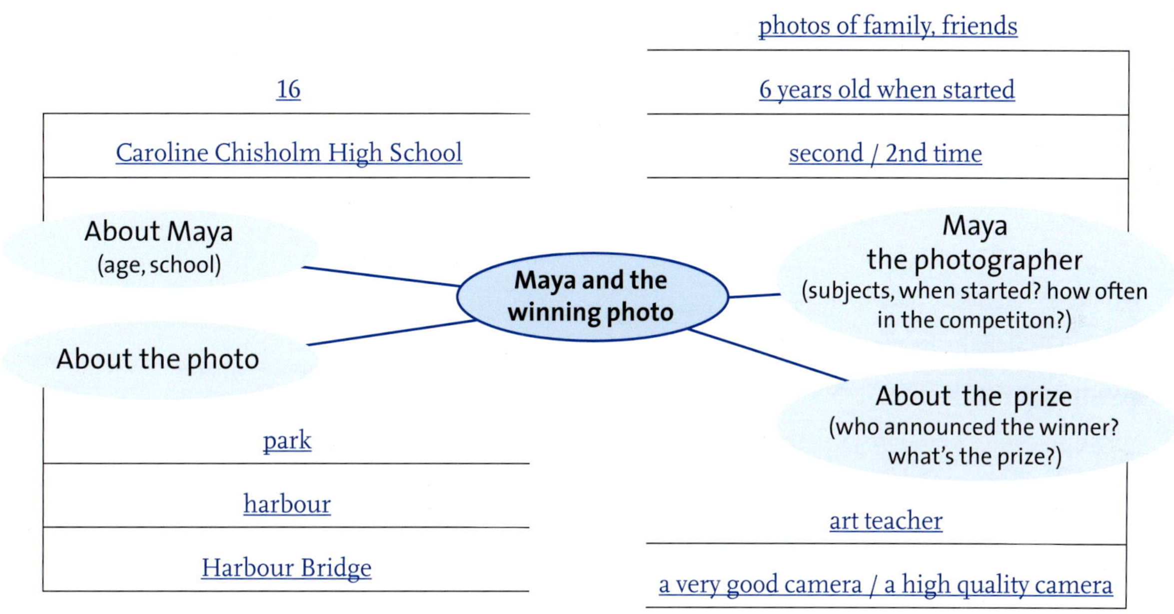

LANGUAGE

1 WORDS A report about the photos

It was surprising that so many people were interested in the photo competition. We received more than 200 photos from 152 students. We divided the photos into different groups. Nearly half of the photos were of Australian natural sights: the blue sea with the high waves, the fish that live in the reef(s) or animals that can only be found in Australia. A high percentage of the photos show Australian everyday life: a party at someone's place, people spending their free time outdoors, a barbecue at the beach. One photo even shows a young couple getting married at the beach in Sydney. There are others of the beautiful Australian desert. Because of the number of photos, we had to organize three rounds to find the winner.
For the last round we invited the art teachers to help us make our decision. They gave us important advice on how to choose the best photos. It wasn't easy. We wanted to avoid choosing a photo which looked like the famous pictures of Australia which all the tourists know, but the choice was just so large!

2 GRAMMAR A day in Maya's family

a)

2 We all have breakfast at 8 o'clock.

3 Sue and I catch the bus to school / go to school by bus at 8.30.

4 My mum goes to work at 8.45.

5 My mum comes home from work at 3.30.

6 Sue and I come home from school and do our homework at 4 o'clock.

7 We all have tea at 6.30.

8 My mum and dad watch TV from 7.30 – 10.30. (Sue and I don't watch TV.) We read books.

b)

Mögliche Lösungen:

I usually get up very early in the morning.

I have breakfast together with my mum.

I don't sleep very long on a normal day of the week.

Lerntipp **Aussagen, Verneinungen und Fragen im *simple present***

- Vervollständige die Tabelle. Die Lösungen findest du auf der letzten Seite dieses Lösungshefts.
- Denk dran: „He, she, it, das -s muss mit!"

	Positive Form	Negative Form	Frage
(to) watch	I watch	I don't watch	What do you watch?
	he watches	he doesn't watch	What does he watch?
(to) see	you		What
	he sees	John doesn't see	
(to) read	I		
	Sue		

3 GRAMMAR Maya is this year's winner

In 2000 our school started organizing photo competitions once a year. Every year there was a happy winner. This year in April the students had to hand in their photos. Like every year you could take part with one or more photos. A team of art teachers and students looked at all the photos and chose the best eight. That was hard work, says Lesley, one of the students. Still, they managed to do it and they finally had just six photos to choose from. Of course, they didn't know the names of the students who had taken them.

The last round was the hardest because all the photos were really brilliant. In the end they picked one photo which looked at this year's topic in a very special way. Congratulations to Maya.

4 GRAMMAR The morning before the announcement

Last Thursday I was terribly nervous because I knew that the winner of the photo competition would be announced at lunch break. I usually don't like getting up early in the morning, but last Thursday I was the first in the bathroom. And I had time to enjoy a really good breakfast. A fantastic start to an exciting day! Every day after morning lessons I spend some time chatting with my friends. But last Thursday I went to the assembly hall right away.

When the art teacher said my name, I couldn't believe my ears at first, but after the first shock everything turned out to be fine.

MEDIATION

1 A photo competition

Mögliche Lösung:

1 Man muss das Foto zusammen mit der Kurzbeschreibung, Details zur Aufnahme (wann und wo), Name, Adresse, Telefonnummer und einer Bildunterschrift auf dem Foto einsenden. Die Mindestgröße beträgt 1 MB.

2 Einsendeschluss ist der 10. Oktober um Mitternacht. Jeder ab 16 Jahre darf teilnehmen. Das Foto muss mindestens 1 MB groß sein. Jeder darf nur ein Foto pro Monat per E-Mail einschicken.

3 Man kann eine Kamera gewinnen, die $ 500 wert ist.

4 Ein Foto wird nicht zugelassen, wenn es mit der Post geschickt wird.

5 Das Foto wird in der nächsten Ausgabe des Magazins zusammen mit dem Namen des Fotografen veröffentlicht.

2 In the shop

Mögliche Lösung:

Julia Danke, dass du mit mir in den Laden gehst. Bei solchen Einkäufen fühle ich mich mit meinen Englischkenntnissen noch nicht sicher genug.

Assistant Hello you two, how can I help you?

Julia OK. Sag ihm, dass ich einen neuen Fotoapparat kaufen möchte, weil mein alter nicht mehr funktioniert.

Maya She'd like to buy a new camera because her old one doesn't work anymore. (2P)

Assistant What kind of camera would you like to buy?

Maya Er fragt, was für eine Kamera du kaufen möchtest. (1P)

Julia Sag ihm doch, dass ich eine Kamera suche, die gute Fotos macht und dennoch nicht so teuer ist.

Maya She is looking for a camera that takes good photos but isn't too expensive. (2P)

Assistant OK, I understand, I can show you some good cameras. Just a minute.

Maya Er sagt, er zeigt uns gleich einige gute Kameras (1P)

Assistant Here you are: this X 400 is a good camera. Take a look at the display. It's quite large.

Maya Also, diese X 400 ist eine gute Kamera. Schau dir mal das Display an. Es ist ziemlich groß. (3P)

Julia Mir gefällt die Kamera. Fragst du bitte, wie viel sie kostet.

Maya My friend likes the camera. How much is it? (2P)

Assistant It's $450,

Maya Sie kostet $450. (1P)

Julia Frag mal, ob er noch andere ähnliche Kameras hat, die er uns zeigen kann und die nicht ganz so teuer sind.

Maya Do you have any other cameras of this kind that cost a bit less? (2P)

Assistant Here's one for $350.The quality is nearly the same but it's not as light and the display is smaller.

Maya Diese hier kostet $350. Die Qualität ist fast so gut wie bei der anderen, aber das Display ist kleiner. (3P)

Julia Also, ich glaube, es ist die richtige Kamera, ich nehme sie.

Assistant OK, I've already understood. It's a good choice. Let me give you an extra battery as a present.

Maya Er hat schon verstanden. Du hast eine gute Wahl getroffen. Er gibt dir noch eine extra Batterie als Geschenk dazu. (3P)

Maya That's very kind of you, thank you very much. Bye-bye.

Julia Bye!

WRITING

Young Australians and animals

Mögliche Lösung:

The four photos each show a young person with one or more animals.

Photo one shows a young woman with a dolphin, in the second photo you can see a lot of kangaroos with a young boy. In photo three there is a young woman with a monkey on her back, and photo four shows a girl with a lamb.

I think all the photos are beautiful. Photos one, three and four show friendships between people and animals. In these photos you can see that the people aren't afraid of their animals but want to help them.

My favourite photo is number three, because it shows only a part of the young woman and the monkey. You can see the background but it is not important for the photo. The girl is carrying the monkey very carefully. Maybe the monkey is ill. For me this photo shows how people and animals can live together in Australia.

SPEAKING

03 Charts about the competition

Hello everybody,

I'd like to present you some information on the number of students who took part in our photo competition in the last three years.

The first bar chart shows you all the students that took part each year. It also compares the number of girls who took part to the number of boys. As you can see 70 students took part three years ago, 52 girls and 18 boys. Two years ago 84 students took part, 56 of them were girls and 28 were boys. Now let me come to last year's competition: this year more students took part in the competition than ever before. You can see that 113 students entered photos, 65 girls and 48 boys.

So we can say that the competition has grown from year to year and that a lot more girls have taken part than boys. But as you can see the number of boys who took part in the competition last year rose more than the number of girls. Perhaps this is a change which will continue next year too?

Now you

Chart A

What the chart is about	Number of students in photo competition this year
Details about the chart	All: 146, girls: 89, boys: 57
My conclusions	More girls than boys

Chart B

What the chart is about	This year's students ▶ How often have they taken part?
Details about the chart	1st time: 78 all students, 57 girls, 21 boys 2nd time: 43 all students, 24 girls, 19 boys 3rd time: 25 all students, 8 girls, 17 boys
My conclusions	A lot of girls take part once, but then don't take part a second time. In fact, very few take part a second time. Not so many boys take part in the competition, but nearly all of them take part a second or even a third time.

Decke die mögliche Lösung unten zunächst ab und formuliere anhand deiner Notizen und dieser Satzanfänge deinen Redebeitrag:
Both charts are about ... / The first chart shows ... / So there were ...
The second chart is about ... / It shows in detail ...
Let's have a closer look at the figures. / ... and ... for the first/second/third time.
The chart shows that there are many more ... than ...
It also makes clear that ...
Vergleiche anschließend deinen Beitrag mit der möglichen Lösung.

Mögliche Lösung:

Welcome to my presentation about the number of students who entered the photo competition this year.
The first chart shows that there were 146 students in all, 89 of them were girls and 57 were boys. That means that a lot more girls took part in the photo competition than boys.
The second chart looks at how often students take part in the competition.
It shows in detail how many students took part for the first, second or even the third time. And it's divided into bars that show the number of girls and the number of boys.
Let's have a closer look at the figures:
78 students, 57 girls and 21 boys, took part for the first time.
43 students, 24 girls and 19 boys, took part for the second time.
25 students, 8 girls and 17 boys, took part for the third time.
The chart shows that there were many more girls than boys taking part for the first time. It also makes clear that a lot of girls only take part once, but nearly all the boys take part a second and even a third time. There are only few girls who take part a third time.

READING

1 Missing headings

1	D	2	C	3	B	4	E	5	A

2 About the text

1 one of the oldest instruments in the world, was played by the North Australian Aborigines

2 Eucalyptus trees

3 finding a living tree with hollow branches / the right kind of wood

4 didgeridoos from abroad or made of plastic

5 take lessons at a school, then go on practising at home

LANGUAGE

1 WORDS Who or what is it?

1 orphan An orphan is a child who hasn't got any living parents.

2 ancestor An ancestor is a member of your family who lived in the past.

3 (to) wash the dishes 'To wash the dishes' is to clean the plates, cups, knives and forks after a meal.

4 (to) apologize 'To apologize' is the same as 'to say sorry'.

5 (to) recommend When you recommend something to another person, you talk about its advantages. You can recommend your camera if you think it's a really good one.

6 (to) introduce sb. To introduce somebody to another person is to say his/her name and give some information about him/her.

7 (to) repeat 'To repeat' something is 'to say it again'.

2 GRAMMAR Ron was on the radio

Ron said that he was 16 years old and lived near Perth together with his family. He said that he loved sports and that he was in the Australian football team. He said that he didn't play every week because he didn't have much time. He said that he wanted to play at least twice a month in the future.

3 GRAMMAR Jill left a note

Mum Hello Matt, is Jill at home?

Dad No, she isn't. But I found a note. It said that she was at Jane's house. She wouldn't be home for tea. They were still working on their presentation because they hadn't finished it yet. But she thought it would be really good. They were going to present it to us on Tuesday evening.

Mum Oh yes, I remember. When will she be back? Did the note say anything?

Dad Yes, it did. The note said she would be back by 8 o'clock.

Mum That's OK. Thanks and see you later. Bye.

Dad Yes, bye.

Lerntipp **Zeitenverschiebung in der indirekten Rede**

Für die **Bildung der indirekten Rede** musst du bei der **Zeitenbildung** sicher sein.

- Sieh dir die Übersicht im Grammar File 4 S.149 in deinem Englischbuch an.
- Erstelle eine Tabelle wie hier angegeben und füge die richtigen Formen von zehn Verben deiner Wahl ein. Nimm auch unregelmäßige Verben. Schreibe die Tabelle in dein Lernheft.
- Übe die Verschiebungen der Zeiten, indem du die *Can you ...?*-Übung S.163 unten in deinem Englischbuch löst.

	Present ▶ past	**Will-future ▶ would + infinitive**	**Can ▶ could + infinitive**	**Going to-future ▶ would + infinitive**	**Present perfect ▶ past perfect**
(to) watch	she watches ▶ she watched	she will watch ▶ she would watch	...	...	...
(to) be	she is ▶ ...	she ...	...		
(to) go	...	...			

WRITING

A surfing accident

Mögliche Lösung:

Last Monday Joe, Jim and Ann, three close friends from Canberra, went surfing near Sydney. When they arrived at the beach, they got changed quickly and went into the water. They enjoyed surfing a lot and the waves were ideal that day.

After some time, the waves began to get higher and higher. Joe thought it was getting too dangerous, so he decided to stop surfing and stayed on the beach but Jim and Ann carried on.

After a while Ann came out of the water, too. Where was Jim? Joe and Ann both tried to spot Jim, but they couldn't find him. They were very worried, so at 3.30 pm they called the lifeguards.

Two lifeguards went out in a boat to look for Jim. Joe and Ann stayed nervously on the beach waiting for news.

After about 20 minutes the lifeguards found Jim and returned with him to the beach. He had been too far out in the ocean. He couldn't get back to the beach, because the waves were too high. Now he was safe though. That was the most important thing for the three friends.

SPEAKING

I can tell you more

a)

Mögliche Lösung:

A Hi! When did you arrive?

B I arrived 10 days ago.

A Wow, that sounds good. By the way, my name is Leon.We arrived yesterday.

B Hi, I'm John. You're German, right?

A Yes, I come from Saarbrücken, that's in the west of Germany. Where are you from?

B I'm from Glasgow, Scotland. Have you been camping before?

A Yes, we go camping every year. This is our first time here. What about you?

B I love camping, too. This is our third time here. And the weather has always been great.

A Do you know where the pool is?

B Sure, it's near the reception, we can walk over to the pool if you like.

A Maybe later. What about a disco or a café, is there a nice place to go in the evenings?

B There's a nice café on the campsite it's just opposite the supermarket. And there's a disco every Friday evening just outside the campsite. It's great. It's only about five minutes' walk.

A I'd like to go swimming in the sea, is it far?

B I want to go to the beach in half an hour. We can go together if you like.

A Good idea. I'll go and get my towel. See you in 30 minutes, John.

B See you!

b)

Mögliche Lösung:

A Hi! When did you arrive?

B I arrived 10 days ago.

A Wow, that sounds good. By the way, my name is Laura. We arrived yesterday.

B Hi, I'm Jenny. You're German, right?

A Yes, I come from Chemnitz, that's in the east of Germany. Where are you from?

B I'm from Cardiff in Wales. Have you been camping before?

A Yes, we go camping every year, but this is our first time here. What about you?

B This is our third time. But this year the weather has been bad so far, so much rain! And it's been really cold. I hate camping. What about you?

A I really hate camping too. I'd like a holiday in a hotel more. What about you?

B Me too. You can relax in your room or in the hotel and if the weather is bad, there's always a lot to do in a hotel.

A Where would you like to go?

B I'd love to go to different places every year, I want to get to know the big European cities like Paris, Barcelona or Vienna. Where would you like to go?

A I really like staying at the sea because I love swimming and I like eating fish!

B Listen, I'd love to have an ice-cream. What about you? We could go and get one from the shop.

A Good idea. I'll just get my money. See you in a minute, Jenny.

B See you!

READING

Who says what?

a)

Paul thinks that work experience makes you more confident.

Tony wants to help young people look for a job.

Nora thinks it's important to like your job.

Lea says that finding a job is easier if you've already done some work experience.

Paul didn't know what he wanted to do after school.

Lea says it's good to hand in any references you have.

Nora thinks that work experience can help you decide what subject you want to study.

Paul applied for a position along with a lot of other people.

Lea thought that work experience should be paid.

Lea says you should tell companies about your work experience when you apply.

b)

1 they liked the way he worked, let him work on his own

2 had part-time job

3 (–) no money, (+) many companies look for people with work experience, can help you find out what you don't want, you can add your reference to your letter of application, learning about teamwork, communication and relationships

LANGUAGE

1 WORDS Your jobs mind map

a)

Mögliche Lösungen:
Wenn du mehr Wörter gefunden hast als gefordert, zählen diese pro Eintrag 0,5 Punkte extra.

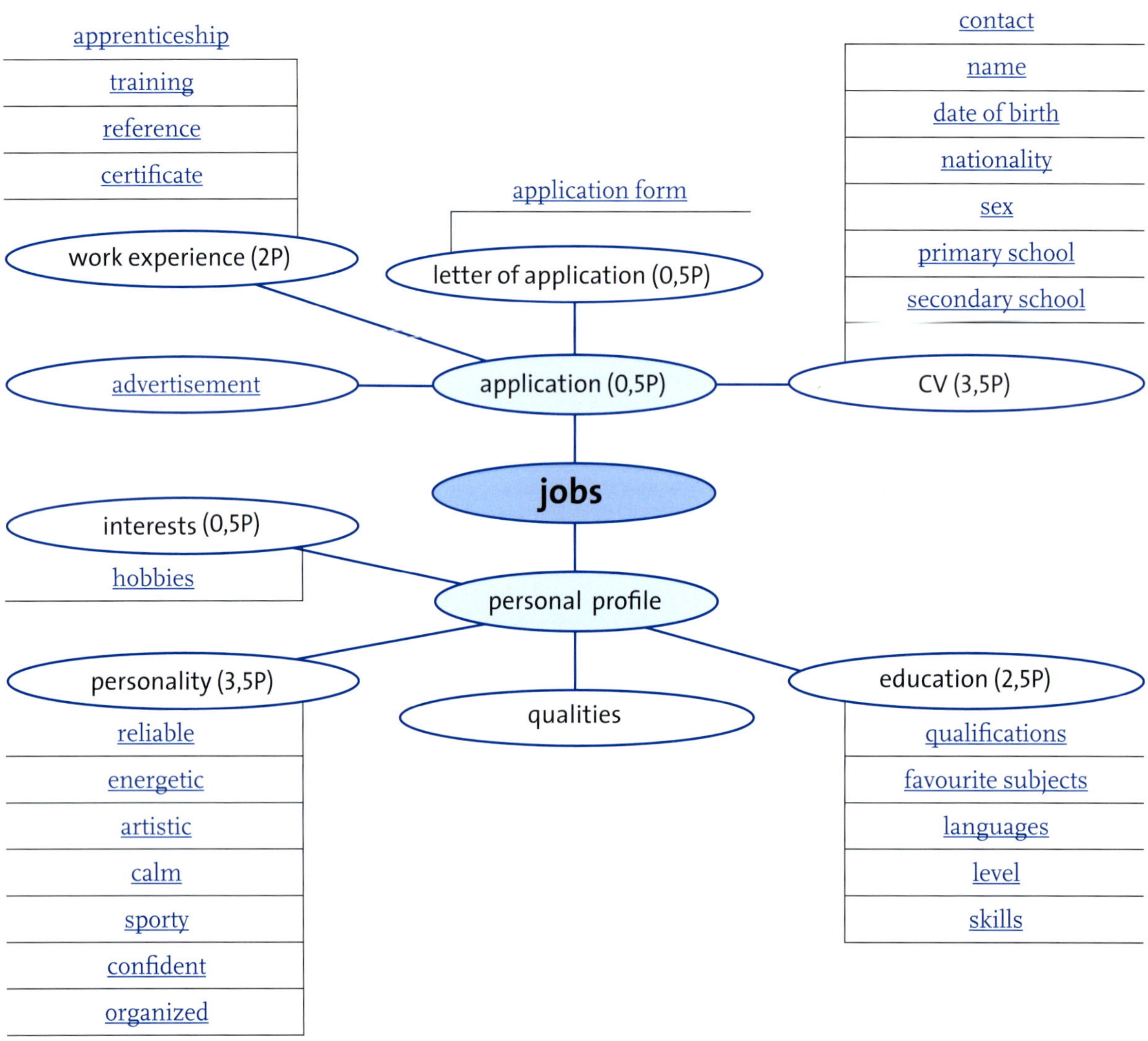

b)

Mögliche Lösungen:

I'm writing a letter of application to a company I really want to work for.

My sister got a very good reference from her last boss.

You have to do three years' training before you can work as a vet's assistant.

I saw an interesting job advertisement in today's newspaper.

2 GRAMMAR Paul's interview at the zoo

1 Paul said that he had been working at the zoo for a few months now.

2 He said that he could start the apprenticeship as soon as we wanted.

3 He added that he liked working with our animals very much.

4 He also said that he got on well with the other zookeepers.

5 He told me that he would work hard if he got the apprenticeship.

WRITING

7 Glasgow Road
Bristol BS15 3LA
(1P)

Alice Spring
St. John's Residential Care Home
4 New Garden Street
Bristol BS1 3AD (1P)

4 November 2011
(1P)

Dear Ms Spring (1P)

I am writing about your advertisement in the Sunday in Bristol of 2 November. I would like to apply for the job at St. John's Residential Care Home. (2P)

I am 16 years old and have very good IT skills. As well as using the computer at home, I have learned a great deal about IT at school. Last term I organized an extracurricular group after school for younger students to help them to use the internet better. I have also taught my grandparents to write e-mails, so I have experience working with older people too. (5P)

I could start after Christmas and am available on Monday, Wednesday or Thursday afternoons. (2P)

Thank you for your time. I look forward to hearing from you. (1P)

Yours sincerely (1P)

Sue Evans

Sue Evans

STUDY SKILLS

Individuelle Lösungen

Lerntipp **Bewerbungsschreiben üben**

Du kannst nun zu deinem Lebenslauf ein Anschreiben auf Englisch verfassen. Achte darauf, alle deine Erfahrungen und Fähigkeiten zu erwähnen, die für die Stellenausschreibung nützlich sein könnten.

LISTENING

Are you happy with your job?

04 1 Terry and Alice

Terry Good morning and welcome to today's show, Radio Today. I'd like to give a very warm welcome to all of our listeners out there, and err, we have a themed week on the topic: are you happy with your job? And every morning between 10 and 11, I'll be interviewing a different person on this topic. And today I'm interviewing Alice who has her own shop. – Erm, Alice have you always been happy with your job?

Alice Err, no Terry I haven't actually, erm, I'm thirty years old now, and yeah my career's going well now. I've got my own boutique, but when I was sixteen, I just didn't know what to do after school. So first of all I just started working at my father's shop, a radio and TV shop, erm, and I just, you know, first of all I, I didn't like radios or TVs, erm, I wasn't interested in the topic, but also I was just working with my family all the time, and that just was not for me. So I stopped working for my father and moved out of the family home and what followed was a bit of a weird period, to be honest.

Terry So how did you find out which job was best for you then?

Alice Well after I'd moved out I started work in a supermarket, and that really gave me a lot of time to think about what I was really good at. You know, my interests, what I really wanted to do, and I talked to a lot of people, that really helped. And I finally applied for a job in a boutique and became a successful shop assistant, erm, and I found out that the manager was happy with my work and that sort of egged me on even further.

Terry And, erm, something else, are your working hours important to you?

Alice Well, erm, now that I am own boss, erm, yes working hours are important for me definitely, but you know after seven years of just doing courses, and, and thinking about what I wanted to do, I decided I don't want to be a millionaire, but I want to be my own boss, so you know, I don't have many holidays, I close the shop for three weeks in the late autumn and I have a relaxing holiday then, that is important to me, erm but I am so happy in my job, it's so fulfilling that I don't really mind the working hours because I've sort of made my hobby my job, if you see what I mean.

Terry Yes, yes. Okay Alice, thank you very much indeed.

Alice That was a pleasure Terry, thank you for having me.

a)

E, A, F, C, B; D wird nicht benötigt.

b)

	True	False
1 Alice had always wanted to work in a TV shop.		✔
2 Alice moved out of her parents' home because she had problems with her parents.		✔
3 When Alice worked in the supermarket, she tried to find out her strengths.	✔	
4 Alice wants to be a millionaire one day.		✔
5 Alice does not go on holidays very often.	✔	
6 Alice is still looking for a fulfilling job.		✔

05 2 Terry and Harry

Terry Hello, good morning, I'd like to welcome all of our listeners out there to today's programme, Radio Today. I'm Terry Cooper and today on the show, I'll be interviewing Harry, he's only 28 but he's already written a book about how to get the best job. Good morning Harry.

Harry Err, good morning Terry.

Terry Um, could you just tell us first of all, how did your career start exactly?

Harry Oh right, erm, well, erm, when I first left school I started working in a careers office, and I was doing secretarial jobs, erm, for about three years. Then I got the chance to do some special training to become a careers advisor and I also did this job for a few years and I actually advised hundreds of young people, some of them who wrote me letters to thank me for my help, and without boasting I still get some letters off these people. Erm, after a while I decided that I wanted to help more young people, so I started working part-time so I would have time to write this book, and this book is all about helping young people find the best job for them.

Terry Right, and how did you get the idea of writing the book?

Harry After working with so many young people, I started seeing that ... two people aren't the same, every single person is individual, so, erm , I started thinking of different ways that people can find the perfect job for themselves.

Terry OK, OK that's very interesting, and, erm, what was the most important step in your career?

Harry Erm, I think it was just getting out there and finding some work because that's how I found out what I personally liked to do.

Terry And have you stopped working as a career advisor?

Harry Err, I still work a little bit, I work part-time but I do focus mainly on the book and going out there, doing talks and advising young people.

Terry OK, what information can readers find in your book, and, and what won't they find?

Harry Well, err, the book, it's basically a guide that helps you through the jungle of job applications.

Terry OK.

Harry Erm, it's a practical book, erm, it has lots of funny pictures and it also has cartoons in there to make you laugh because what I found with young people is they don't just wanna read and read and read, they need something that focuses them and, erm, something that's interesting.

Terry OK, and what won't they find in the book?

Harry Well, like I just mentioned, they won't just find pages and pages of information that will make them go to sleep, erm, they won't find things that are telling them that is the one particular way to do things.

Terry Right, so it's lively and engaging.

Harry It's lively, it's engaging, well I hope it's lively and engaging and, erm, the response like I said that I've had off young people has been very positive.

Terry And what makes you happy in your job above all else?

Harry Erm, the best thing for me in my job is making other people happy, and getting people, and giving them the advice, and pushing them down the road for their perfect job.

Terry Great, OK Harry we'll have a little break here with some music and after the break we come back and we'll listen to Harry's tips.

a)

1 people wrote letters / from the letters he got

2 He wanted to write a book.

3 to start working / to find his strength

4 a guide through the jungle of applications / how to find a job

5 pictures and cartoons

6 He can help other people / give them advice.

Terry And, err, we're back after that little break there, err, back here with Harry, who, as I say is only 28 but has already written a book about how to get that, err, the best job, and, err, so Harry, what are your tips?

Harry Well, err, the 'shoulds' of getting a good job that you really like, err, are you should take time to find out what you're really interested in, and find out your strengths.

Terry Right.

Harry In the book there is a game which helps you to match your interests and strengths with different jobs. Find out your other skills by volunteer work, or by doing work experience. Talk to other people about their jobs whenever possible. Apply for jobs. Practise interviews, every job interview is practice for the next one.

Terry Right, right.

Harry So, get more confident talking about yourself. The 'should nots' are, well, don't worry if you don't get a job straightaway, but just don't sit at home waiting for the phone to ring, you should volunteer for work, or, I don't know, try to learn a foreign language. Do training, if possible and don't think that a good job is always a job which pays you a lot of money.

Terry Hmm, alright Harry, thank you very much indeed, that's, that's great advice.

Harry Thank you.

Terry I'm sure all of our young people out there will very much appreciate that, and, err, get out there and buy that book and give it a good read, and, err, and take Harry's tips and advice on board.

Harry Available at all good bookstores at £7.99.

Terry Of course, and well worth the money. Thank you very much indeed Harry.

b)
1C, 2A, 3B, 4E, 5F

LANGUAGE

1 WORDS Getting by in English

1 The teacher expects us to do our homework.

2 To date only five students have volunteered.

3 I don't mind sitting next to the window.

4 I waited ten minutes before the shop assistant served me.

5 I am determined not to start smoking.

2 WORDS Different jobs

a)

1 Somebody who works in a kindergarten is a childcare assistant.

2 Somebody who cooks in a restaurant is a chef.

3 Somebody who often helps people who want to lose weight by doing more sport is a fitness instructor.

4 Somebody who repairs cars is a mechanic.

b)

1 A dentist's assistant is somebody who helps the dentist with his work.

2 A driving instructor teaches people how to drive.

3 A nurse is a person who works at a hospital.

4 A coach is somebody who helps people to become better, e.g. a swimming coach trains the swimmers.

3 WORDS Just look at my letter!

I'm so happy! I just got an an invitation for a job interview. It's for an apprenticeship in a hotel. I think there'll be quite a few candidates though so I must try to impress the manager. I'm going to work out what I want to say during the interview. I know that I'll have to talk about myself, about my qualifications but also about my weaknesses. And I'll have to think of some questions to ask! Oh, I also need to go to the shops to look for some suitable clothes and I'm going to wear a tie.

4 GRAMMAR Parents!

1 My mum told me to do my homework every day.

2 She told me not to talk during lessons.

3 She asked me to get up earlier in the morning.

4 My dad asked me to have a good breakfast every day.

5 He told me not to stay out too long at night.

6 He told me to study with my friends in the afternoon.

5 GRAMMAR Information for my teacher

1 I asked them what they did on a normal day at work.

2 I wanted to know at what age they had decided on their career.

3 I asked them what they liked most about their job.

4 I wanted to know what their next career steps would be.

5 And I asked them if they had ever thought about doing another job.

6 GRAMMAR A talk with the neighbour

I told our neighbour that I was doing a project for school about jobs and that I was interested in talking to a builder about his work. He said that he worked for a big building company in Liverpool. He added that he had had his job for over twenty years now. He said that he and the other workers worked outside all day. I told him that I needed the information for a presentation. He thought that it was a good thing to learn about jobs at school. He also said that I could come to see one of the houses he was building at the moment. I said that I would come the following week.

MEDIATION

Talking about an advert

Deine Mutter	Also jetzt gehen wir die Anzeige noch mal zusammen durch, ich habe nämlich nicht alles so genau verstanden. Was für eine Stelle ist genau ausgeschrieben?
Du	Sie suchen jemanden, der in Teilzeit von Montag bis Freitag auf Schulkinder aufpasst und zwar von 16:15 bis 17:15 Uhr. (3P)
Deine Mutter	Und was musst du da genau machen?
Du	Ich muss mich um die Erstklässler kümmern, soll die Erzieher unterstützen und mit den Kindern drinnen und draußen spielen. (3P)
Deine Mutter	Das klingt ja ganz gut. Aber musst du da keine Erzieherausbildung haben?
Du	Nein, aber ich muss schon Erfahrung in der Arbeit mit Kindern haben.
Deine Mutter	Und welche persönlichen Eigenschaften muss ein Bewerber mitbringen?
Du	Man muss zuverlässig, flexibel und sportlich sein und gut mit Eltern, Lehrern und Kindern zusammen arbeiten können. (4P)
Deine Mutter	Wie sieht es denn mit den Fremdsprachenkenntnissen aus?
Du	Man muss gute Englischkenntnisse haben, und zwar sowohl schriftlich als auch mündlich und Kenntnisse in mindestens einer weiteren Fremdsprache haben. (3P)
Deine Mutter	Ich glaube, du könntest dich da bewerben. Ruf doch gleich mal an.
Du	Das geht leider nicht. Man muss sich per E-Mail bewerben. (1P)
Deine Mutter	Und was musst du da noch beachten?
Du	Der Bewerbungsbrief muss auf Englisch sein und man kann auch noch Empfehlungsschreiben beifügen. (2P)

WRITING

A person who loves her job

Musterlösung:

I'm writing about my mother who is a hospital nurse. (2P) She only works part-time. (1P) Sometimes she starts work early in the morning, but very often she has to work late in the evening. (1P) She gives the people in the hospital their meals, washes them and helps them whenever she can. The most important part of her job is talking to the people, showing that she is interested in them and making them laugh. This is difficult because some of the people are really ill and have to stay in hospital for a long time. (7P)
I know that my mum is a good nurse and I know that she likes her job very much although it's sometimes hard work. But she is happy when she can help. (4P)

SPEAKING

06 A job interview

Mr Preston Hello, Josh. How are you?

Josh Fine, thanks Mr Preston.

Mr Preston Please take a seat, Josh. Now, I've read your letter of application and your CV carefully so I already know a few things about you. Could you start by telling me a bit about yourself. Tell me about your school. What do you like about school – and maybe what you don't like about it?

Josh Well, I go to Woodland Secondary School and I'm in my last year at the moment. Although I quite like school, I'm looking forward to finishing in a few months. I'd like to do something with my hands after all that time in the classroom.

Mr Preston And what are your favourite subjects? And why do you like them?

Josh My favourite subject is IT, I like computers. I started working with computers when I was very young. So I know quite a lot about them really. I also really enjoy PE. When I was a little boy, I always played football with my two older brothers. Later I joined a football club where I still play today.

Mr Preston Very interesting, Josh. Now can you explain why exactly you're applying for the apprenticeship here?

Josh As I said, I'm looking forward to finishing school and I'd like to work with my hands. My father always repairs things in our house, and I like helping him. I suppose that's why I want to do a practical job.

Mr Preston Fine, thanks Josh. Have you done any work experience at all?

Josh Yes, we did work experience at school last year. I went to an office but I didn't really like it. You know I love my computer, but I don't think I'd like to work on it all day long. It was a good experience though.

Mr Preston Can you describe your character and your strengths?

Josh I think I'm relaxed but I work hard and I love finding out new things. I think that's important if you want to repair cars because it can often take a long time to understand what's wrong, so you have to keep on trying out new things. And I'm good at working in teams. I learned that from playing football of course.

Mr Preston Now, before we finish, have you got any questions you'd like to ask, Josh?

Josh Yes, I have. How many people work here? And are there only men, or women as well?

Mr Preston Ah, that's interesting. There are 17 of us altogether and, yes, there are some women too! There are two secretaries and my wife works here too.
Right, Josh, That's it for the moment. Thank you very much for the interview. I hope to contact you in about a week to tell you if you've got the job or not.

Josh Thank you very much, Mr Preston.

Mr Preston Thanks for coming. Goodbye.

Josh Goodbye and thank you very much!

07 Now you

Mrs Harris Hello. How are you?

You I'm fine, thank you very much – just a bit nervous. (1P)

Mrs Harris Please take a seat. Now, I've read your letter of application and your CV carefully so I already know a few things about you. Could you start by telling me a bit about yourself. Please tell me about your school. What do you like about school – and maybe what you don't like about it?

You Well, I go to Elisabeth Gesamtschule. I like going to school but I'm looking forward to finishing very soon. I think it's time for a change and I'm really excited about that. (3P)

Mrs Harris What are your favourite subjects? And why do you like them?

You My favourite subject is art. I like working with my hands and making things. (2P)

Mrs Harris Very interesting. Can you explain why exactly you are applying here?

You As I said I'm looking forward to finishing school and I like working with my hands. I've always loved cooking and I am very interested in different foods and trying new things. I also love making things, as I've already said, and I think this might be very useful as a cook. (5P)

Mrs Harris Fine, thank you. Have you done any work experience at all?

You Yes, we did work experience at school last year. I worked in a shop. I thought I would be able to make news clothes and give advice to customers. But it wasn't like that at all. It was very different from what I had expected. (5P)

Mrs Harris Could you describe your character and your strengths?

You I think I'm very creative and I love making new things. I'm also very ambitious. I work hard to get good results. And I love trying new things. I very often cook for my family and friends and they always enjoy it and say they see my talent. That's why I would like to train as an apprentice with you. I can work in a team and can take advice, but working alone is also no problem for me. (10P)

Mrs Harris Ah, that's interesting. Right, that's it for the moment. Thank you very much for the interview. I hope I can contact you in about a week to tell you if you've got the job here.

You Thank you very much, Mrs Harris. (1P)

Mrs Harris OK, thanks for coming. Goodbye.

You Goodbye and thank you very much! (1P)

Lerntipp **Sprechen üben**

Nachdem du das Interview durchgeführt hast, solltest du überlegen, was dir noch schwer gefallen ist. Notiere dir hilfreiche Formulierungen. Wiederhole dann diese Übung in ein paar Tagen noch einmal.

LISTENING

A presentation about graffiti

08 *a)*

Paul Hello, my name's Paul, and in the second part of this presentation we wanted to learn a bit more about graffiti and people's opinions about it. So we asked three different people, a policeman, an art teacher and a seventeen-year-old girl. The questions we asked these people were: What do you think about graffiti? What does graffiti mean to you? And is graffiti an art or a crime? So, let's listen to those interviews first and then I'll give you my opinion on them.

Policeman What do I think about graffiti? Well I can tell you that it takes up a great deal of police time. There's a lot of time wasted on paperwork, we receive a lot of calls in the morning from members of the public, who are understandably very angry. We have members of the public who have had graffiti painted over night, and often it's cleaned away and reappears the next day. It appears in different places, people's homes for instance, but also on official buildings and [in] underground stations and even on the trains. So I think it's perfectly understandable that members of the public are quite rightly angry, I think I would be too. What does graffiti mean to me? Is it art or a crime? Ha, well I can tell you it's a crime, no doubt about it. It's not art, it's just a lot of work for me, I could be doing other things, like catching burglars or something. It's not art, it's a form of vandalism, it's a crime and it costs a lot of money cleaning it up all the time. I can tell you for example, we had a case a few weeks ago where eight people were caught graffitiying on a London Underground. Well, they'll be getting an ASBO that's for sure. What I would like to see is buildings painted with a special paint that you can't spray on. That would save a lot of work.

09 *b)*

Art Teacher What do I think about graffiti? Well, I'm an art teacher so I don't think it's all that bad. In fact I've given the students in year nine a project about graffiti. So what we've agreed on is that there are certain walls in the schoolyard that the students are allowed to perform graffiti on, and this is part of their artwork, and I think it's, it's a form of expression for these students. It doesn't necessarily have to be an expression of opinion; it can be an artistic expression. And I actually think that the work that they've been doing is really very, very good. This sort of work is usually more popular amongst the boys and, um, we've also been discussing and, and hopefully we will visit some of the galleries that show professional graffiti. So graffiti for me, well, it gets a thumbs up!

What does graffiti mean to me? Well, I think it can go both ways. It can be art at some point but it can also be a crime if it's sprayed on private houses, for example, and it shouldn't be, at all, sprayed on historical buildings. I think that if graffiti fits into the area of the city or the place that it is, then it can be an expression of art and actually be quite beautiful because it brings colour to some of the greyness of cities. Um, I think there is a very distinct difference between good graffiti and art, and graffiti which is vandalism. I think that, um, in the future graffiti will be ordered per se or commissioned, and I think famous people will be given jobs to lighten up the cities and express themselves in an artistic and graffiti like manner.

10 ***c)***

Girl Um, well, unfortunately we don't do graffiti at school but I think it will [sic; besser wäre *would*] be a good idea. I first started doing graffiti as a hobby and I practise a lot, on paper and behind, err, my house on this wooden wall. I'd really like to become a famous sprayer one day. I think this is because I can show people how I feel, and it's, well, it's an urban art form to bring people together I think.
I heard of this amazing graffiti artist in the south of Germany, who has been asked to spray graffiti on a church. I think it's a great idea, that's what I'd really like to do. So, it really inspires me, you know, to see this art form and I can practise it anywhere, and I can develop my skill and I'll just get better and better and then maybe one day I can paint on one of the buildings. I think graffiti also makes places more interesting for young people, so yeah I really like this art.
What does graffiti mean to me? Well, I think it's art but only if it's a real picture. I think there should be legal places where spraying is allowed. There are places for skateboarders so there should be special places for sprayers too. I think, well for me, it can help me relate to other people. This is such a positive thing for me to do. Um, is it a crime? Well, I don't think so.
For many people graffiti is not a crime anymore, this has changed. Graffiti may become real art in the future.

Paul So as you can see there are many, many different views on graffiti. For some people it's something they're very, very interested in, for other people it can be seen as a crime and something that's quite an irritation. So, my opinion would be, graffiti is a very, very interesting art form, it adds a lot of colour to the city and it makes people think in different ways.

a)

1c), 2b), 3b)

b)

1 with students from year nine, some walls in the school yard for graffiti, they did very well, boys like this kind of work better, they want to visit galleries
2 private houses and old buildings
3 if it fits into the area, if it brings colours to the cities
4 graffiti will be ordered, famous people will be given jobs to make the cities more colourful

c)

1 She would like to do graffiti at school.

2 She practises graffiti on paper and behind her house on the wall.

3 Through her graffiti she wants to show people how she feels.

4 There is a German artist who does graffiti on the wall of a church.

5 She hopes to become a famous graffiti artist.

6 In her opinion, graffiti makes places more interesting for young people.

7 She thinks spraying should be allowed in certain places.

8 Paul concludes that some people are interested in graffiti, but others think graffiti is a crime.

LANGUAGE

1 WORDS New graffiti at the station

1 I was surprised when I passed the station the other day. What had happened? Someone had graffitied one of the walls.

2 I was very impressed by the graffiti, but it was surprising how many people didn't seem to notice the new graffiti as they walked past.

3 Weren't they interested in graffiti? Or were they just in a hurry so that they didn't see anything at all?

4 It's depressing that people don't notice what is around them.

5 I really like graffiti but I'm a bit worried about the person who sprayed it. If the police catch them, they will have to pay a large amount of money and get an ASBO.

2 WORDS John talks about what happened yesterday morning

I always set the alarm clock for 7 o'clock. When the alarm clock rang yesterday, I turned it off as usual and then I fell asleep again because I was still very tired. Time went by quickly and when I finally woke up again it was 7.50! Oh dear – what was I going to do? I had hoped that my mum would give me a lift to school but she was already busy in her office. So I ran to the bus stop, but of course I had missed the bus. I ran home again to get my bike. Perhaps I would still make it to school on time.

3 WORDS Using new words

Mögliche Lösung:

The news from Afghanistan is rather worrying.

They had vandalized the school building and were punished for it.

When she visited her boyfriend's family, she behaved really well.

My sister is going to get married. Her wedding is next weekend.

When I go shopping for my mum, I always ask for a receipt.

When I worked on my computer yesterday, I forgot to save my work.

He is addicted to computer games.

4 GRAMMAR Graffiti in a church

a)

built, living, showing, sprayed on, visiting

b)

Eine katholische Kirche im Süden Deutschlands, die 1961 erbaut wurde, hat Dank eines örtlichen Graffiti-Künstlers ein neues Aussehen.

Als die Idee das erste Mal vorgeschlagen wurde, waren die Leute, die in dem kleinen Ort leben, gegen das Projekt.

Als er seine Idee für ein neues Aussehen der Kirche präsentierte, gelang es ihm, den Ort für sich zu gewinnen. Das große Graffiti sollte über dem Eingang die Jungfrau Maria mit dem Jesuskind zeigen.

„Aber schauen Sie hier: Die leeren Sprechblasen, die an diese Wand gesprüht wurden, sind bereits mit Gebeten und Wünschen gefüllt. Dies zeigt uns, dass die Menschen, die unsere Kirche besuchen, sich daran beteiligen.“

Lerntipp **Partizipialsätze**

Partizipialsätze können Relativsätze ersetzen. Beim Verständnis von Sätzen mit einem **present participle (-ing-Form)** oder einem **past participle (3. Form des Verbs)** solltest du immer an diese Möglichkeit denken. Dies ist bei Übersetzungen besonders wichtig.

Zusätzliche Übung

Ersetze die folgenden Relativsätze durch ein Partizip.

1 The woman who spoke first in the discussion was Mrs Summer.
2 The graffiti that was sprayed on the wall near the train station was very political.
3 The artist who explained the art of graffiti was one of my father's friends.

MEDIATION

A voucher for an audio book

Es handelt sich um einen Gutschein für drei Hörbücher. (1P)

Man besucht die Homepage der Firma, erstellt sich ein Benutzerkonto, wählt aus über 20,000 Büchern aus, lädt sich die gewählten Bücher herunter und speichert sie. (5P)

Das Herunterladen ist für 20 Tage kostenlos. (1P)

Man erhält pro Monat ein Hörbuch, für das man £ 8,99 bezahlen muss. Nur wenn man innerhalb der ersten 20 kostenfreien Tage kündigt, muss man nicht bezahlen. (3P)

1 The woman speaking first in the discussion was Mrs Summer.
2 The graffiti sprayed on the wall near the train station was very political.
3 The artist explaining the art of graffiti was one of my father's friends.

SPEAKING

11 A school trip

Sandra So, Adam, what do you think about our school trip? Would you prefer a trip to Edinburgh or would you rather join this outdoor adventure camp in Wales?

Adam Well, my sister went to one of those camps and she didn't really like it. That's why I'd prefer to go to Edinburgh. I think a sightseeing trip would be brilliant.

Sandra I don't agree. I think it would be a great opportunity for our class to go on this adventure camp. We'll learn so much about the group and about ourselves.

Adam I agree with you. But can't we learn about each other if we're together in Edinburgh? We'll be in groups in the hostel for example.

Sandra I don't think that it's the same really. If we went to this adventure camp, we'd do things together and we'd learn a lot about teamwork. I'm sure that this would be a great opportunity for all of us.

Adam Maybe you're right about the social aspect. But I'm sure we'd have a lot more fun in a city like Edinburgh.

Sandra Sorry, but I don't understand what you mean.

Adam Oh come on, Sandra. There are so many good places to go in Edinburgh, just think of the clubs. We could go dancing in the evenings.

Sandra I see what you mean, but I don't think that we'd be allowed to go.

Adam Yeah, maybe you're right about that.

Sandra So do you agree to go on the adventure camp in Wales?

Adam Yes, OK, we should give it a try.

Now you

	Journey	How long?	Where to stay	Costs	Free time	Sightseeing	Evening programme	...
Berlin	by train	five days	hostel city centre	€250 + pocket money	go shopping	learn about German history	go to theatres, cinemas, cafés	
London	by plane	four days	families outside London	€340 + pocket money	get to know about the British way of life, go shopping	visit places from English lessons, see famous sights	stay at home with families	

A What do you think about our school trip? I'd love to go to London because we could visit the places we've learned about in our English lessons and see famous sights.

B I don't agree. I'd like to go Berlin because I haven't been there yet. I think it would be a great idea for our class to go to Berlin really because we could go sightseeing or shopping during the day and go to theatres, cinemas or cafés in the evenings. And we could learn so much about German history.

A That's a good point. Maybe it would help our marks in history. But what do you think about staying in a hostel? I like the idea of going to London because we would stay with families outside London and get to know more about the British way of life and we could also go shopping. I don't like hostels.

B I see what you mean, but the hostel would be in the centre of Berlin, which means that we could go out in the evenings and have fun. If we stayed with English families, we would have to stay at home most evenings.

A I agree with you. I'd also like to go out in the evenings.

B And what about the costs? We'd be away for five days and we could go to Berlin by train, which would make it cheaper. London is very expensive.

A Yes, that's true. You're right about the costs and we'd also need pocket money, don't forget that. The trip to Berlin would still be cheaper, and Berlin is also really interesting.

B You're right. So, Berlin it is – do you agree?

A I do. I can visit London on my own in a few years' time anyway.

READING

Who said what?

a)

Mayor: 1, 7, 10

Steve: 2, 6, 9

Sarah: 3, 5, 11

b)

Mögliche Lösung:

I think we need youth clubs. (1P) Young people aged between 12 and 17 must have a place where they can meet. (2P) A youth club is a good place because you don't necessarily need money when you go there. (2P) And a youth club always offers a lot of activities that you couldn't do on your own. (2P) I go to a youth club once a week. (1P) I'm a member of the drama group there. (1P) And I help younger kids with their homework. (1P)

LANGUAGE

1 WORDS A crossword

									9 ▼		
				3 ▼		2 ▶ 5 ▼	B	U	S	Y	
	1 ▼			D		C			H		
	T	4 ▶	B	E	H	A	V	I	O	U	R
	R			S		S			P		
	A			E		H	7 ▼		L		11 ▼
6 ▶	S	T	O	R	E		C		I		S
	H			V			O		F		E
		8 ▶	R	E	C	E	I	P	T		C
							N		I		R
									N		E
		10 ▶	O	V	E	R	N	I	G	H	T
											L
					12 ▶	M	A	I	N	L	Y

2 WORDS Paraphrasing

a)

1 spring

2 prayer

3 exchange rate

4 troublemaker

b)

1 If you are not allowed to smoke in a club, that is because smoking is banned.

2 People who are under 18 years old are under age.

3 Valuables are things that cost a lot of money or mean a lot to you.

4 Trash is another word for rubbish.

3 GRAMMAR In the new school cafeteria

a)

The new school cafeteria is used by both teachers and students.

The new school cafeteria is run by the students themselves.

Although teachers are against it, sweets are sold in the new school cafeteria.

b)

The old door was painted.

The windows were cleaned.

The curtains were put up.

c)

As you can see, some changes have been made in the last two months.

The tables and chairs have been put in different positions so that there is more room in between.

The walls have been painted in bright colours to make the cafeteria friendlier.

A piece of graffiti has been done on one of the walls.

d)

More things will be done in the next few weeks.

The new lamps can be installed on Friday.

New plants and flowers must be bought.

Meals can be chosen from the menu.

4 GRAMMAR The new youth club

Every month a lot of young people are attracted to the youth club by the activities we offer.

Since February this year two new workshops have been created.

Last month it was girls in particular who were involved in many of the workshops.

In the next few weeks also boys must be found for some special activities.

A new computer must be bought. The old one doesn't work anymore.

And – for July a big summer party has been announced.

WRITING

School uniforms should be introduced at German schools.

Mögliche Lösung:

a)

Outline

1. Introduction

   School uniforms in UK and other countries

2. arguments for (+)

   2.1 make life easier: no more bullying

   2.2 make life cheaper: not expensive, designer clothes

   2.3 make schools safer: you know who belongs to the school

   2.4 make better atmosphere: students identify with school

3. arguments against (–)

   3.1 school uniforms don't stop bullying: still possible with other things like mobile phones, ...

   3.2 not really cheaper: parents buy uniform plus other clothes, school uniforms are expensive

   3.3 students don't like uniforms

4. Conclusion

   + school uniforms > school atmosphere > very important

b)

Written discussion

Students have to wear school uniforms in Great Britain and in many other countries. Should school uniforms be introduced in Germany too? Lots of people think that school uniforms make life easier and cheaper, so they should be introduced, but there are also some arguments against changing the system in our country.

First, an important argument for school uniforms is to do with bullying. Bullying other students because of their clothes could be stopped because all the students would be wearing one uniform. School uniforms could also save parents money because they wouldn't have to buy expensive clothes for their children.

Another argument for school uniforms is that they could make schools safer because you can tell who is a student at the school and who isn't.

Third, students who wear a uniform might be encouraged to identify more with their school. A uniform can give young people who wear it a sense of belonging to a group, which can be very important.

On the other hand, school uniforms don't stop bullying completely. Students who want to bully other kids will find something to bully them about. This can be a cheap mobile phone or the family's car.

→

It is only partly true that school uniforms are cheaper. The families have to buy the uniform and clothes that kids can wear at weekends and during holidays. In some cases, the uniforms themselves can be very expensive and have to be replaced as children grow.

It is also important to remember that some students might not like wearing a school uniform and having to do so might have a negative effect on their attitude towards school.

After looking at both sides of the argument, I believe that school uniforms should be introduced at German schools because there are a lot of important advantages, especially for the atmosphere at school. However, I don't think that students should be made to wear a uniform if they don't want to. The students should agree on the style of their school uniform, e.g. this could also be a school T-shirt or sweatshirt.

Bewertung und Punkte bei Schreibaufgaben

Dein Text enthält ...	**Punkte**
1. Einleitung: Einführung ins Thema	4
2. Thesen und Argumente der Fürsprecher	6
3. Thesen und Argumente der Gegenseite	6
4. Schlussfolgerung: deine Meinung nach Abwägung beider Seiten	4
	20

LISTENING

12 At the airport restaurant

Jane Hi, my name's Jane and I'm, err, I'm going to South Africa today, I'm flying to Johannesburg. I'm visiting my cousin and her husband and their little daughter, she's just ten months old. They live in the northern suburbs of Johannesburg, my cousin's husband's pretty successful, he, he works for a British company there and they've been there for about two years. I've never flown before, but this is a direct flight and there's almost no time difference with the UK so that's really great, I hopefully won't get any jetlag. I can't wait to do some sightseeing in, in South Africa, I, there's this Kruger Park, which is meant to be really good. I really want to get to know the country, I've heard a lot about South Africa, especially about apartheid. I'm quite interested in, in the history of South Africa but I'm also really eager to see the beautiful landscape. So this trip for me is, it's a mixture of, of family and sightseeing. I'm going to do some babysitting for two days when my cousin and her husband go on a short trip, just the two of them. It's a present for my cousin, I think she's been a little stressed after the first few months with her baby.

Florian Hello, I'm Florian! I'm waiting for my plane to the USA. Well, yes, I'm, I'm pretty excited because, err, it's the first time I've ever been to America. In fact it's, it's the first time I've ever been to an English speaking country, erm, the only time I've ever been on a plane was, err, about two years ago when I went to Spain with my parents. But now, err, first New York, and from New York I'm going to take a plane to San Francisco, I'm going to stay for, for six months and most of it will be, erm, working and erm I guess there, there won't be much time for sightseeing, I mean, and erm, I'm, I'm pretty excited because erm I'm going to work in the US, it's, it's not a sightseeing tour, I'm err, I've got a job in a residential home, you know, working with, erm, elderly people and so, and I think that's quite challenging, erm, I know there's, err, there's not much time for other things but, erm, I'm, I'm glad it's not in a big city like, err, San Francisco or so because, erm, if you work in a place that is big and noisy and crowded, err, I guess it's difficult to meet people and make friends but, erm, this is a small town, it's about 50 kilometres from San Francisco. You know, erm, if you have a job it's much easier to learn English and, erm, that is an important part of my stay in the US, you know, learning English, because, erm, later on I would like to work in some international firm or so, erm, and nowadays you don't get anywhere without English, so after these six months I would really like to speak English fluently, you know. Well, I do hope there's going to be some time for sightseeing, I mean there's, there's a lot I'd like to see, err, you know, San Francisco and, and L.A. perhaps, I don't know, but, erm, anyway, on my way back, there I'll have three days, erm, in New York to look at Manhattan, erm, at least before going back to Germany, but if there's the possibility to do things like, I mean, err, on the West Coast I've heard you can do surfing there for example, I'd really like to do a surfing course, that's, that would be great, but first of all, I'd like to arrive there safely and, erm, see the place where I'm going to live for the next six months.

Brian Um, yes, um, yes, my name is Brian, yes, um, I'm a businessman. I'm flying to Mumbai, I work for a German company that sells, err, clothes, some of which are produced in India. Well, we sell T-shirts and, err, sweatshirts, jeans, blouses, mostly for the younger generation. Um, I'm flying [sic; besser wäre *I fly*] to Mumbai usually about once a month, stay for about four days or so, just under, um, and visit the companies of course where our clothes are produced and talk to our business partners in India about projects or problems and the future, um, I fly quite often, yes, so it's rather normal for me, bit like taking a train you might say. On a long-haul flight I would probably occupy myself with some work or something of that sort on my laptop, um, I usually go to India, you know, just for business, so I don't often to get to see much of the country when I'm there but I would love to, you know, um, bring my family with me one day, um, when I can have some time off for a long holiday, maybe let's say a month, a few weeks, four weeks, a month, you know and really get to know the country, would be lovely, yes.

a)

1 Who is Jane going to visit? *(3 people)*	her cousin, her husband and their daughter
2 Where in Johannesburg does her cousin live?	in a northern suburb
3 What do you know about her cousin's husband? *(2 things)*	pretty successful works for a British company
4 How long have they been in South Africa?	for about two years
5 How often has she been on a plane before?	never
6 Why does Jane not expect to have a jet lag?	almost no time difference with the UK
7 What does she want to do in South Africa? *(4 things)*	go sightseeing, visit Kruger Park, get to know the country, learn about its history, see the beautiful landscape
8 What's her present for her cousin?	two days of babysitting

b)

1 Florian has been ...	a) to America before.	
	b) to an English-speaking country before.	
	c) on a plane before.	✔
	d) to many different countries before.	

2 During his stay Florian ...	a) will spend most of his time working.	✔
	b) will go sightseeing a lot.	
	c) will work in a hotel.	
	d) will stay in San Francisco.	

3 Florian wants ...	a) to visit Washington, D.C.	
	b) to live in a big city.	
	c) to learn as many languages as possible.	
	d) to learn English and work at the same time.	✔

4 Florian has already decided ...	a) to do a surfing course.	
	b) to go to Los Angeles and San Francisco.	
	c) to stay in New York for three days.	✔
	d) to visit the West Coast.	

c)

1 Brian is flying to Mumbai.

2 He works for a German company.

3 The clothes they produce are sold mainly to young people / the younger generation.

4 Brian usually goes to India once a month.

5 When he is in India, he visits the Indian companies / talks to his business partners.

6 On a long flight he usually works / works on his laptop.

7 One day he wants to visit India together with his family / to get to know the country.

8 If he's not on a business trip, he wants to stay for four weeks / one month.

LANGUAGE

1 WORDS City words

a)

Mögliche Lösungen:
Wenn du mehr Wörter gefunden hast als gefordert, zählen diese pro Eintrag 0,5 Punkte extra.

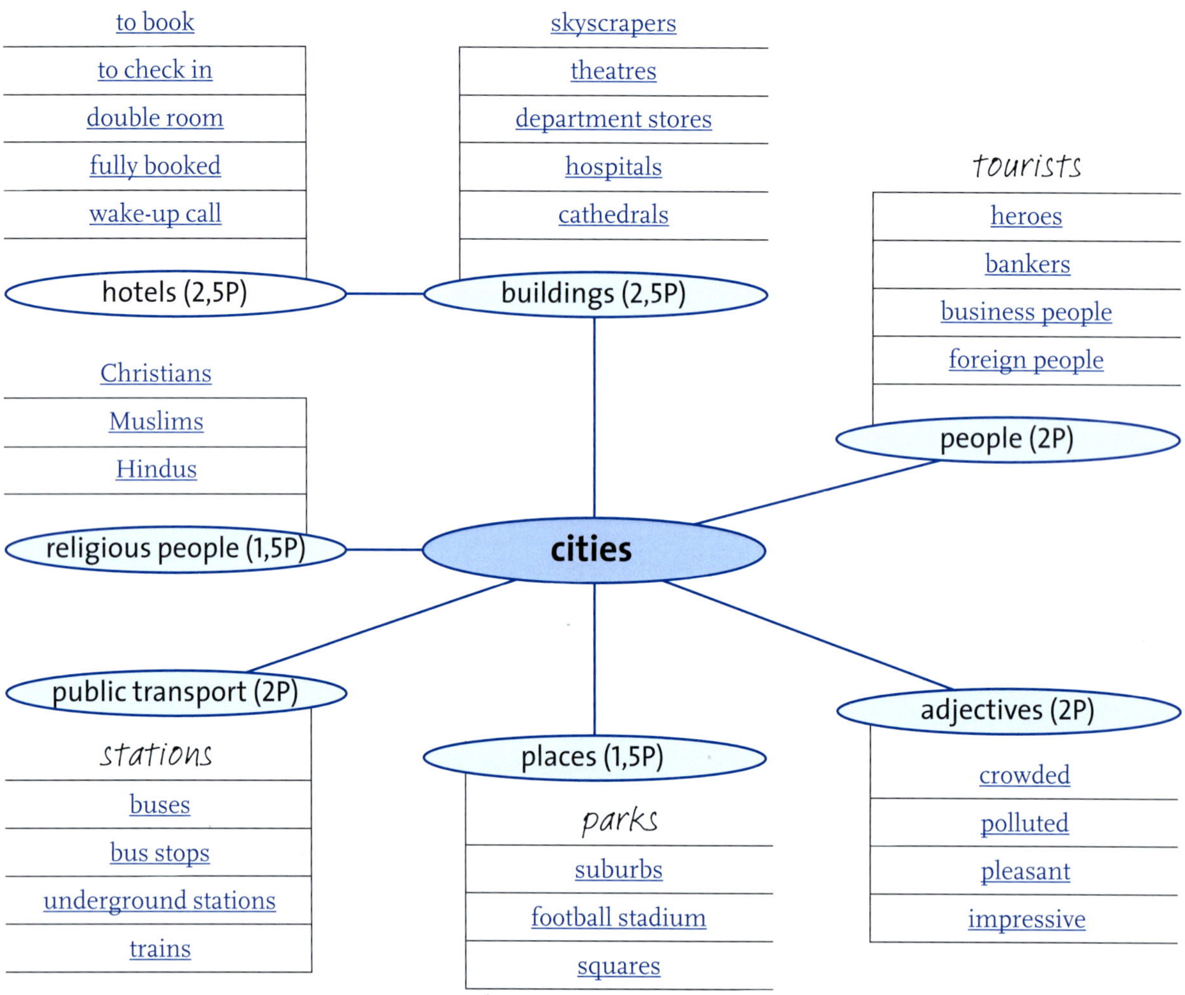

Lerntipp **Wiederholung von Vokabeln**

Mindmaps sind eine gute Methode, um neues und bereits bekanntes Vokabular zu wiederholen. Schreibe die Mindmaps sorgfältig in dein Lernheft und wiederhole sie von Zeit zu Zeit. Du kannst sie dann auch immer auf den neuesten Stand bringen, indem du neue Vokabeln ergänzt. Beispiele für Themen: **holidays**, **all about jobs**, **media**, **sports**, **clothes** ...

b)

1 In big cities there's lots to do – you can visit a cathedral, a shopping centre and a museum all in one day.
2 I like the smell of the trains in underground stations.
3 Families very often live in suburbs of big cities.
4 Many tourists visit my city to watch a match in the crowded football stadium.

2 WORDS Our unforgettable class trip

a)

useful, useless, usual, homeless, central, noisy, industrial

b)

2 Our hotel was very central.

3 Hamburg is an industrial city.

4 I think a guidebook can be very useful.

5 The streets were very noisy.

6 Look – the man over there is homeless and has to live on the streets.

3 GRAMMAR What if ...?

1 If Dad let me work at the supermarket for a few hours a week, simple past	**A** you wouldn't have to run for the bus. would + Infinitiv
2 If you got up earlier in the morning, simple past	**B** she won't have enough time to do her homework. will-future
3 If our neighbours go on holidays in August, simple present	**C** I will look after their two cats. will-future
4 If my sister goes shopping this afternoon, simple present	**D** we wouldn't understand them. would + Infinitiv
5 If everyone in the class does their homework regularly this term, simple present	**E** we will be allowed to watch a film at the cinema before the holidays. will-future
6 If the teacher didn't explain the rules in maths so well, simple past	**F** I could earn some extra money. could + Infinitiv

1	F	**2**	A	**3**	C	**4**	B	**5**	E	**6**	D

Now you

Mögliche Lösungen:

If I didn't chat to my neighbour so much during the maths lesson, I would get better marks.

If Susan is able to save enough money, she can go on holiday with her friend.

If this rucksack was cheaper, I would buy it right away.

If our class decides to go on a school trip, we will definitely go to London.

MEDIATION

At the doctor's

Deine Mutter Bitte sag ihr, dass ich Fieber habe und ich mich einfach nicht wohl fühle.

Du My mum has got a temperature and she feels sick. (1P)

Ärztin Does anything hurt?

Du Tut dir irgendetwas weh? (1P)

Deine Mutter Ich habe Kopfschmerzen und mir ist kalt.

Du She's got a headache and she is cold. (1P)

Ärztin I see. When did it start?

Du Wann hat das angefangen? (1P)

Deine Mutter Vor zwei Tagen, als ich auf einmal nichts essen konnte.

Du It started two days ago when she suddenly couldn't eat anything. (2P)

Ärztin Well, I don't think it's anything serious. You should drink about two litres of water, fruit juice or tea every day. No coffee please. And don't stay in the sun too long.

Du Sie glaubt nicht, dass es etwas Ernstes ist. Du sollst ungefähr zwei Liter Wasser, Fruchtsaft oder Tee pro Tag trinken, aber bitte keinen Kaffee. Du sollst nicht zu lange in der Sonne bleiben. (2P)

Ärztin These pills should help you. Take one pill half an hour before every meal, three times a day. If you don't feel better in three days, I want to see you again.

Du Diese Tabletten werden dir helfen. Du sollst dreimal täglich eine Tablette eine halbe Stunde vor dem Essen nehmen. Wenn du dich in drei Tagen nicht besser fühlst, sollst du nochmals kommen. (2P)

Deine Mutter Vielen Dank.

Ärztin You're welcome. All the best.

WRITING

My trip to ...

Last spring I went on a class trip to the Black Forest. One day we visited Freiburg. Freiburg is a city with a population of about 200.000 people. It's near the border with France and Switzerland. (4P)
There is an old university in Freiburg, so there is a big student population too. We went on a sightseeing tour with a tourist guide. He was really nice – the girls liked him because he was very good-looking. (5P)
The guide showed us all Freiburg's important sights: the two main towers, the house with the oldest pub in Germany and of course the Münster with the great square around it. (4P) We went inside the beautiful Münster and some of us also went up the tower where you can enjoy a breathtaking view of the city. (2P)
I loved the square around the Münster with the colourful market where you can buy different kinds of fresh fruit and vegetables. (2P)
Freiburg is a very young and beautiful city. Because it is not as big as Frankfurt or Berlin, it is easier to get to know, which I liked a lot. (3P)

SPEAKING

Describing a photo

This is a photo of a young man with his car somewhere in the countryside. (1P) In the foreground you can see the young man standing in front of his grey car. (1P) Behind the car you can see fields with flowers, trees and there are some hills in the background. (2P) I think there is part of a house behind the forest. (1P)
There are no other people in the photo. (1P)
You can't see the road. The car is probably parked at the side of the road. The bonnet is open and you can see the engine. (3P) The young man is on his mobile. (1P) He looks worried. I think there is something wrong with his car and he is trying to get some help. (3P) At the moment he isn't talking, I think he's listening to the person on the phone. Maybe the person is telling him that he can't come to help him right away and this news worries him because he will have to wait for quite a long time. (3P)

READING

Life in South Africa today

a)

Mögliche Lösung:

Things that have changed for the better:

Electricity and water in houses, Jo'burg modern with good shopping centres, black people can go to university, more kids at school, better equipment in schools, books for students at school, people are not as poor, people appreciate each other

Things that still have to be changed for the better:

No jobs, a lot of crime, police don't care about crime, 50 students in one class, high dropout rate at school

b)

Education has improved in the last few years. (1P) More children can go to school. (1P) The equipment is better in the schools. (1P) Sometimes there are 50 students in one class and the dropout rate is high. (2P) Today every black student can go to university and study. (1P) However, there are still many boys and girls who would like to go to school longer but can't because the family doesn't have enough money. (2P)

LANGUAGE

1 WORDS Combining words

a)

collect impressive autographs

send an official message

rent a small flat

fancy glamorous movie stars

fight for political freedom

hate crowded trains

b)

Mögliche Lösungen:

She collects impressive autographs.

The government will send an official message.

My brother only rents a small flat.

My sister fancies glamorous movie stars.

This party fights for political freedom.

I think public transport is a good thing, but I hate crowded trains.

2 WORDS Find the correct word

1 After the factory had closed, the unemployment rate rose dramatically.

2 It's cheaper to use public transport than to go by car.

3 In some places there is a lot of rubbish lying around – such places are polluted.

4 I wasn't feeling well, so I went to the doctor. He gave me a prescription for some pills.

5 I met an old friend yesterday. He looked completely different, so I didn't recognize him first.

6 There were so many people who wanted to go to the concert. We had had to queue for more than one hour before we got the tickets.

7 Can't we take the bus? I don't fancy walking all the way.

3 GRAMMAR I would have ...

a)

A I saw a man stealing a book in the bookshop, but I didn't do anything.

B I would have told the manager.

A When I was in London, I went to the British Museum.

B Museums are boring. I would have gone to Madame Tussaud's (instead).

A I saved all my pocket money and bought myself a new skateboard.

B I would have bought a new surfboard.

A When I was 12 years old, I decided to learn Latin.

B I would have decided to learn Spanish (instead).

b)

Mögliche Lösung:

A I didn't tell my parents about my bad marks in maths.

B I would have told them.

4 GRAMMAR If ...

1 If Tom went to Australia for a year, his parents would visit him in the summer holidays.

2 If the Millers hadn't seen the advert for the house in the newspaper, they wouldn't have moved to this beautiful area.

3 If the teacher tells us the date of our test, I will start preparing this afternoon.

4 Our cat Minca would be very unhappy if we left her alone over the weekend.

5 If the new student in our class had talked talk about his problems, my friend and I would have helped him.

6 If Susan didn't want to study Spanish at university, she wouldn't go to Mexico for a year.

7 If I meet John this afternoon, I will ask him about the project.

8 The three boys wouldn't have started fighting if the others had left them alone.

5 GRAMMAR If, if, if ...

a)

1 yes

2 no

3 yes

b)

1 If the students stay quiet, ...	A the teacher wouldn't have given them any homework.	
	B the teacher will not give them any homework.	✔

2 If the Millers moved from Bristol to London, ...	A Cindy would live in London.	✔
	B Cindy would have lived in London.	

3 If I had left home a bit earlier, ...	A I will catch the bus.	
	B I would have caught the bus.	✔

MEDIATION

A conversation about Berlin public transport

Frau Gonzales We're flying to Berlin-Schönefeld. How do we get to the city centre from the airport?

Du Sie fliegen nach Berlin-Schönefeld. Sie wollen wissen, wie sie vom Flughafen in das Zentrum kommen. (2P)

Deine Mutter Am besten nehmen sie die S-Bahn. Wo ist denn ihr Hotel?

Du It's best if you take the train, it's called the "S-Bahn". Where is your hotel? (2P)

Herr Gonzales I think it's right in the city centre at a square called "Alexanderplatz". Do you know it?

Du Er glaubt, dass es im Zentrum ist, in der Nähe eines „Alexanderplatzes". Kennt ihr den? (2P)

Dein Vater Natürlich kenne ich den. Das ist sehr gut, denn man kann direkt mit der S-Bahn dorthin fahren und man braucht überhaupt nicht umsteigen.

Du My dad knows the place. He says it's good because you can go there directly by S-Bahn without changing. (3P)

Frau Gonzales That's fine. Now what about the tickets? Where do we get them and how much are they?

Du Sie möchte wissen, wo sie die Fahrscheine bekommen und wie viel sie kosten. (2P)

Dein Vater Am besten kauft man die Fahrscheine schon vorher übers Internet. Es gibt besondere Tickets für Touristen, die 2, 3 oder 5 Tage genutzt werden können. Man kann dann fahren so oft man will, sogar bis nach Potsdam.

Du It's best if you buy the tickets online. There are special tickets for tourists which can be used for 2, 3 or 5 days. You can use them as often as you like. You can even go to Potsdam. (4P)

Herr Gonzales That's great. Thank you so much for your information. I think it's time for a cup of coffee. Come on.

SPEAKING

13 My holidays

Moritz

My topic today: My holidays in Arcachon in the south-west of France

I'm going to divide my presentation into 5 sections:

Firstly: where Arcachon is

Secondly: how we got there

Thirdly: about the area of Arcachon

Then: our tents and our campsite

And finally: my opinion about my holidays

Firstly, where Arcachon is

Now, please have a look at this map of Europe ... Here you can see France, Paris, the Atlantic Ocean, in the south there is the border to Spain.

This map shows you France on its own, Arcachon is in the south-west. Look, here you can see Bordeaux, which is only 45 kilometres away.

And here you can see where Arcachon is situated. It's right next to the Atlantic Ocean. Here you can see Cap Ferret and this is the famous "Dune de Pilat" which you can see on the next photo.

2 Let me come to my second point. I'd like to tell you how we got to Arcachon.

We left Stuttgart at eight in the morning on Wednesday 15th August in our car. On this map you can see Stuttgart. We, that's my parents, my sister Jana (she's 13) and me.

After two hours we crossed the border into France. The border is here on the map – but as you can see there was still a long way to go.

We drove through France. I really liked the journey because the weather was lovely and there was a lot to see. In the evening we stopped at a small hotel and the next morning we carried on. We arrived in Arcachon at 4 pm on Thursday ... Great.

Next, the area of Arcachon

As I've already mentioned, Arcachon is right on the Atlantic Ocean. It's a nice town with beautiful houses, actually a lot of them are villas and there are many wonderful beaches.

You can sunbathe, swim in the sea, go surfing or diving, there's something for the whole family.

Have a look at my photos: here you can see one of the famous beaches in Arcachon, and here's one of the many diving schools, as you can see there are old and young people who are interested in diving and of course there are always people who just want to lie in the sun, as you can see in this photo.

If you like going out in the evenings, you can go to one of the brilliant restaurants and after that about ten discos are waiting for you and your friends.

Next our tents and our campsite

Finally, I'm going to talk about the campsites. There are several campsites in Arcachon. Ours was really big and very near to the beach. In my opinion, it's the best campsite in Arcachon. We had reserved so we got a really good and large place for our two tents, a big one for my parents and a smaller one for my sister and myself. This photo here shows you our two tents. As you can see, there is room for the whole family in my parents' tent. But we only use it if the weather is bad. Normally we are outside the tents all day. This photo here shows you the campsite in the small forest. You can see that there is a lot of shade because of the trees. If you're camping, shade is important because otherwise it will get too hot in the tent at night. The campsite is ideal for families with children because it's near to the sea and there's a swimming-pool where the younger children can swim and play. Have a look at this photo, isn't it nice?

...

To end my talk, I'd like to present my personal opinion. As you might imagine I love camping. And I loved being on the campsite in Arcachon.

The campsite is modern, big and you have everything you need. It's near to the sea – you can walk to the beach. I love the freedom of staying on a campsite. You do nearly everything outside. And I love being at the seaside. Arcachon is a great place because you can do so many things there.

Maybe you'll go there one day too. Thanks for your attention. Please feel free to ask questions or comment on anything I've said.

Outline + visual material	Useful phrases
Introduction	My topic today ... / I'm going to divide my presentation ...
Where Arcachon is: map of Europe and of France	Firstly, ... / Here you can see ...
How we got there: map	On this map you can see ... / As you can see ...
The area of Arcachon: photos	As I have already mentioned ... / ... is right on ... / Have a look at ...
Tents and campsite: photos	Next, ... / Finally, ... / Have a look at ... / this photo shows you ...
Opinion	To end my talk ... / Thanks for your attention ... / Please feel free to ask questions or comment on anything I've said

Lerntipp **Präsentationen üben**

Trage deine Präsentation einem Freund / einer Freundin oder deiner Familie vor. Wenn du kleine Schwächen von dir bereits kennst, bitte die Zuhörer besonders auf diese Punkte zu achten.
Solche Punkte können z. B. sein: Blickkontakt halten, die Einbeziehung von Medien, langsames und deutliches Sprechen oder auch wie überzeugend du etwas vorträgst.

Now you

Individuelle Lösungen

Who said what?

a) *Write the numbers of the sentences under the photos. Be careful: there are two more sentences than you need. (9P)*

Mayor

Steve

Sarah

1 Thank you for the money.

2 Come and join our club.

3 I liked thinking about the building.

4 The youth club is not for the younger kids.

5 We got to know other youth clubs in Britain.

6 It's good for young people to be a member of a youth club.

7 Two architects built the building with the help of the young people in the area.

8 We will not sell any alcohol in the club.

9 We are looking for volunteers.

10 We had to close the old youth club.

11 There is so much to do in our youth club.

b) *What's your opinion? Do we need youth clubs? Write a short text of about 70–80 words. (10P)*

LANGUAGE

___/40

1 WORDS A crossword

___/12

Complete the sentences and fill in the crossword.

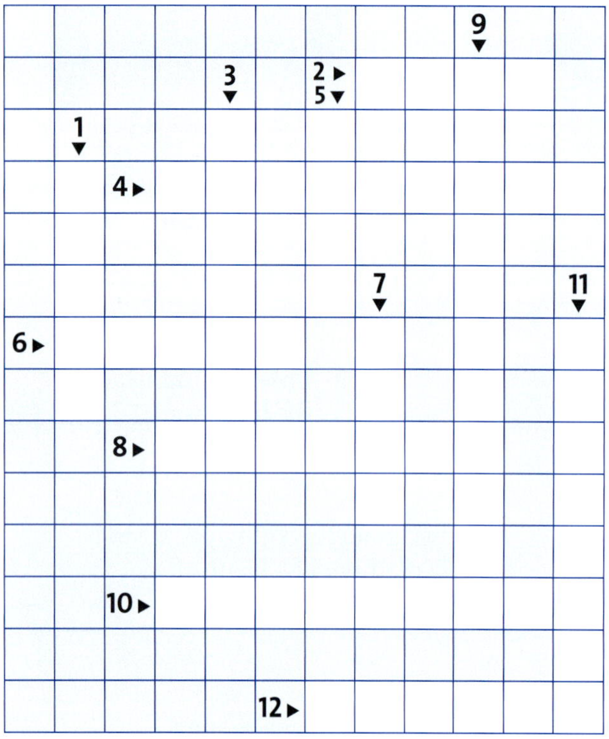

Across

2 I can't go out tonight. I'm too ... .

4 She is very polite and friendly. Her ... is excellent.

6 You should ... this bottle in a cool place.

8 When I go shopping for my mum, I always ask for a ... in the shop.

10 It was too late to go home and already dark, so we stayed ... .

12 During the day I ... drink water.

Down

1 Another word for rubbish.

3 We've worked really hard. I think we ... a break now.

5 If you don't pay by credit card, you pay ... .

7 Have you got a five-pence ...?

9 Another word for stealing goods.

11 She didn't tell anyone about the present. She ... put it on the table.

2 WORDS Paraphrasing

____ / 8

a) *Which word is described in the phrase or sentence?*

1 This is a place where a river starts.

____

2 If you go to church on Sundays, you will say this.

____

3 If you want to change money into another currency, you must ask for this.

____

4 A word for a person who often behaves badly.

____

b) *How can you explain these words?*

1 ban ______________________________

2 under age ______________________________

3 valuables ______________________________

4 trash ______________________________

3 GRAMMAR In the new school cafeteria

____ / 14

Here is a report about the new cafeteria with information about the ***present****, the* ***past*** *and the* ***future****.*

Bildung des Passivs
Diese Übung passt zum Grammar File auf S. 152 in deinem Englischbuch.

Zeit	Form von **be + past participle (3. Form des Verbs)**	
Simple present	am/are/is	seen
Simple past	was/were	seen
Present perfect	have/has been	seen
Will-future	will be	seen
Modal auxiliaries	can/must/should/ ... be seen	

a) *What is done today? Complete the sentences with the* ***passive (simple present)****. (3P)*

The new school cafeteria ______________________ (use) by both teachers and students.

The new school cafeteria ______________________ (run) by the students themselves.

Although teachers are against it, sweets ______________________ (sell) in the new school cafeteria.

→

b) *What was done last week? Complete the sentences with the* ***passive (simple past)****. (3P)*

The old door ______________________ (paint).

The windows ______________________ (clean).

The curtains ______________________ (put up).

c) *What has been done in the last few months? Complete the sentences with the* ***passive (present perfect)****. (4P)*

As you can see, some changes ______________________ (make) in the last two months.

The tables and chairs ______________________ (put) in different positions so that there is more room in between.

The walls ______________________ (paint) in bright colours to make the cafeteria friendlier.

A piece of graffiti ______________________ (do) on one of the walls.

d) *What will (can/must) be done? Complete the sentences with the* ***passive (future, can/must/should)****. (4P)*

More things ______________________ (will – do) in the next few weeks.

The new lamps ______________________ (can – install) on Friday.

New plants and flowers ______________________ (must – buy).

Meals ______________________ (can – choose) from the menu.

4 GRAMMAR The new youth club

_____ / 6

After two months, the members of the youth club team talk about the work in the youth club. Complete the sentences with the correct forms of the ***passive****. Be careful with the tenses.*

Every month a lot of young people ______________________ (attract) to the youth club by the activities we offer.

Since February this year two new workshops ______________________ (create).

Last month it was girls in particular who ______________________ (involve) in many of the workshops.

In the next few weeks more boys ______________________ (must – find) for some special activities.

A new computer ______________________ (must – buy). The old one doesn't work anymore.

And – for July a big summer party ______________________ (announce).

WRITING

____ / 20

School uniforms should be introduced in German schools

*Choose **one** of the following topics:*

- *Collect ideas for and against school uniforms.*
- *Teens should be allowed to drive at the age of 16.*
- *Teenagers' time online should be limited automatically.*

a) *Use an **outline** to organize your arguments.*

b) *Write a **written discussion** of about **200–220 words**.*

Gliederung (outline) und Erörterung (written discussion)

1. Gliederung (outline)
- hilft beim Ordnen deiner gesammelten Ideen
- erleichtert dir das Schreiben deiner Erörterung
- besteht aus drei Teilen: **Introduction, Arguments, Conclusion**

2. Erörterung (written discussion)
- **Introduction:** allgemeine Aussage, eine Frage oder eigene Erfahrung
- **Present your arguments (FOR or AGAINST):** Bringe deine Argumente in eine logische Reihenfolge und beachte für jedes Argument die folgenden drei Schritte: Führe dein Argument auf, erläutere und begründe dein Argument und gib dann Bespiele, um dein Argument zu unterstützen.
- **Conclusion:** eigene Meinung ohne neue Argumente

- Versuche zunächst selbst, diese Aufgabe zu lösen. Wenn du mehr Ideen benötigst, findest du im Lösungsheft eine **Outline** mit Argumenten. Decke die Musterlösung zur **Written discussion** zunächst ab und vergleiche diese erst hinterher mit deinem eigenen Text.
- Diese Übung passt zum Skills File auf S. 154 und zu S. 59 in deinem Englischbuch.

Klassenarbeit A

Gesamtpunktzahl ohne Speaking	____ / 100	Note ____
Gesamtpunktzahl mit Speaking	____ / 116	Note ____

LISTENING

____ / 20

12 At the airport restaurant

Where are you flying to today?
Listen to three people who have been interviewed for the local radio at the airport restaurant in Frankfurt.

a) *Listen to Jane **once** and answer the following questions. You needn't write complete sentences.*
Press 'pause' when Jane has finished.
Then listen again and complete your answers. (8P)

1 Who is Jane going to visit? *(3 people)*	
2 Where in Johannesburg does her cousin live?	
3 What do you know about her cousin's husband? *(2 things)*	
4 How long have they been in South Africa?	
5 How often has she been on a plane before?	
6 Why does Jane not expect to have a jet lag?	
7 What does she want to do in South Africa? *(4 things)*	
8 What's her present for her cousin?	

b) *Listen to Florian* ***once*** *and tick (✔) the correct answer a, b, c or d. Press 'pause' when Florian has finished. Then listen again and check your answers. (4P)*

1 Florian has been ...	a) to America before.	
	b) to an English-speaking country before.	
	c) on a plane before.	
	d) to many different countries before.	

2 During his stay Florian ...	a) will spend most of his time working.	
	b) will go sightseeing a lot.	
	c) will work in a hotel.	
	d) will stay in San Francisco.	

3 Florian wants ...	a) to visit Washington, D.C.	
	b) to live in a big city.	
	c) to learn as many languages as possible.	
	d) to learn English and work at the same time.	

4 Florian has already decided ...	a) to do a surfing course.	
	b) to go to Los Angeles and San Francisco.	
	c) to stay in New York for three days.	
	d) to visit the West Coast.	

c) *Listen to Brian* ***once*** *and complete the sentences below with 1–5 words or numbers. Then listen again and complete your answers. (8P)*

1 Brian is flying to ________________________.

2 He works for ________________________.

3 The clothes they produce are sold mainly to ________________________.

4 Brian usually goes to India ________________________.

5 When he is in India, he ________________________.

6 On a long flight he usually ________________________.

7 One day he wants to visit India ________________________.

8 If he's not on a business trip, he wants to stay ________________________.

LANGUAGE

____ / 50

1 WORDS City words

____ / 18

a) *Complete the mind map with as many new words as possible. You can add more if you wish. (14P)*

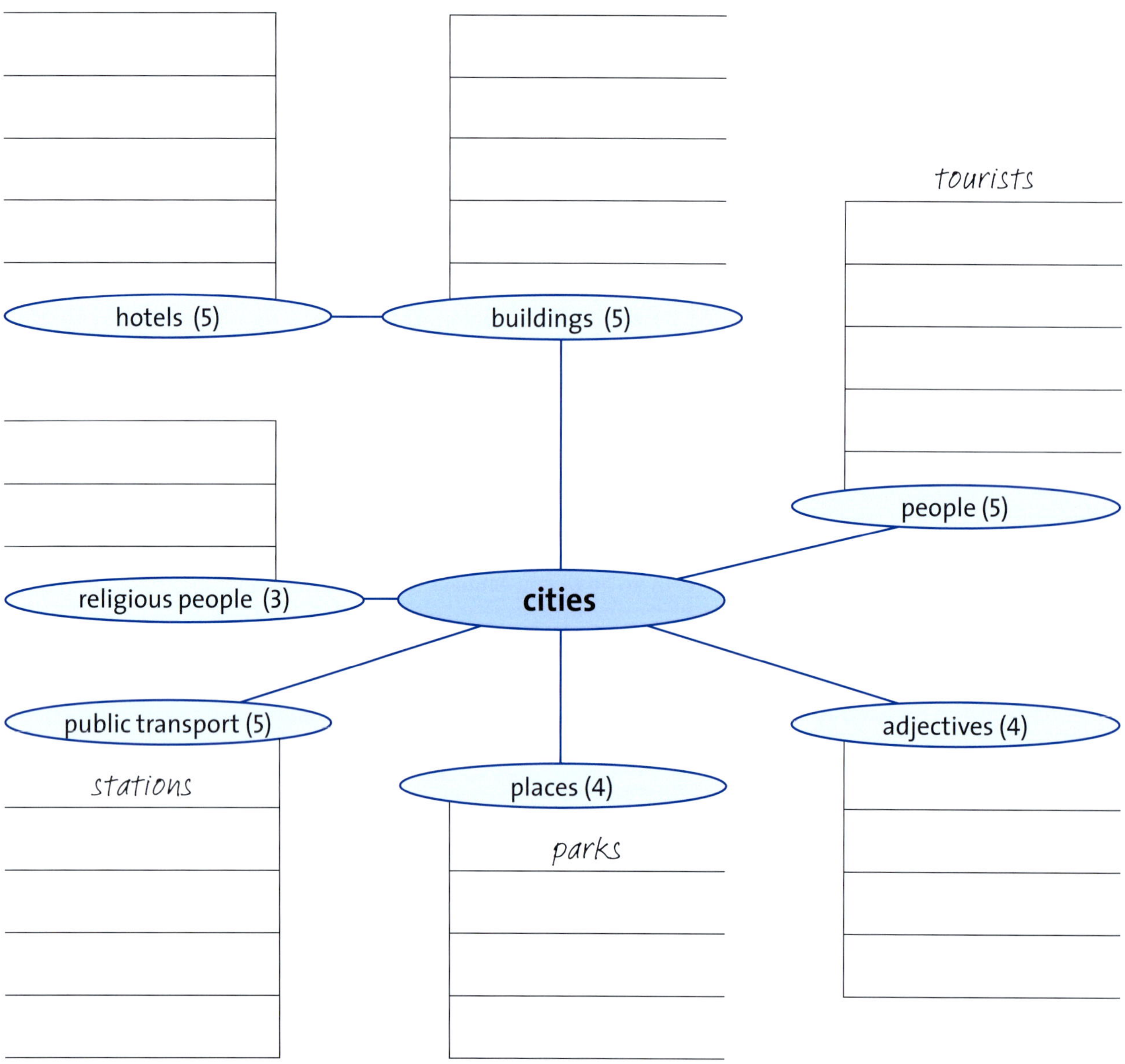

b) *Choose* ***four*** *words from your mind map and write sentences for each one in your exercise book. (4P)*

2 WORDS Our unforgettable class trip

___/ 10

a) Look at the table and make adjectives with endings from the box. (5P)

-able • -al • -ful • -ial • -less • -y

use	
home	
centre	
noise	
industry	

*b) Complete the sentences with adjectives from **a)**. (5P)*

1 I'll never forget our class trip to Hamburg, it's such a beautiful city.

Our class trip to Hamburg was *unforgettable*.

2 Our hotel was near the centre of Hamburg.

Our hotel was very ______________________.

3 Hamburg is an important city for German industry.

Hamburg is an ______________________ city.

4 I often use a guidebook when I am in a new city.

I think a guidebook can be very ______________________.

5 There was such a lot of noise in the streets.

The streets were very ______________________.

6 Look – the man over there doesn't have a home and has to live on the streets.

Look – the man over there is ______________________ and has to live on the streets.

3 GRAMMAR What if ...?

____ / 22

First write the tenses of the if-clauses (1–6) and the main clauses (A–F) into the table. Then match the correct main clauses to the if-clauses. (18P)

If-Sätze – Conditional sentences (type 1 and 2)

Type 1	If-clause: **simple present**	Main clause: **– will-future** **– can/should/must + Infinitiv**
	If I **go** to London,	I **will visit** Buckingham Palace.
Type 2	If-clause: **simple past**	Main clause: **would/could/might + Infinitiv**
	If my sister **went** to Australia,	she **would visit** Sydney.

Diese Tabelle hilft dir bei der Vervollständigung der Sätze. Überlege bei jedem Satz, welche Zeit vorgegeben ist. Du kannst dann in der Tabelle oben ablesen, welche Zeiten zusammen passen. Wenn du dich sicher fühlst, deckst du die Tabelle oben einfach ab und kontrollierst anschließend.

1 If Dad let me work at the supermarket for a few hours a week, ______	**A** you wouldn't have to run for the bus. ______
2 If you got up earlier in the morning, ______	**B** she won't have enough time to do her homework. ______
3 If our neighbours go on holidays in August, ______	**C** I will look after their two cats. ______
4 If my sister goes shopping this afternoon, ______	**D** we wouldn't understand them. ______
5 If everyone in the class does their homework regularly this term, ______	**E** we will be allowed to watch a film at the cinema before the holidays. ______
6 If the teacher didn't explain the rules in maths so well, ______	**F** I could earn some extra money. ______

1		2		3		4		5		6	

Now you

Think of suitable endings and write complete sentences. (4P)

If I didn't chat to my neighbour so much during the maths lesson, ______________________

______________________.

If Susan is able to save enough money, ______________________.

If this rucksack was cheaper, ______________________.

If our class decides to go on a school trip, ______________________.

MEDIATION

___/10

At the doctor's

Veränderung der Person bei Mediation
Beispiel: Tom unterhält sich mit Frau Merkert über eine Wohnung, er spricht nur englisch, sie nur deutsch. Du kannst bei der Unterhaltung helfen, weil du beide Sprachen sprichst.
Tom: **I would like to rent your flat.**
Du: Er würde Ihre Wohnung gerne mieten.

Bei Mediation musst du häufig die Person ändern, wenn du sprichst. Das kannst du in dem kleinen Beispiel oben gut erkennen: aus „I" muss „er" werden, wenn du sprichst, denn Tom möchte die Wohnung mieten und nicht du.

Du bist mit deinen Eltern in Spanien in Urlaub. Deine Mutter fühlt sich nicht wohl, so dass ein Arztbesuch notwendig wird. Die Unterhaltung zwischen deiner Mutter und der Ärztin ist auf Englisch. Du hilfst mit der Sprache.

Deine Mutter Bitte sag ihr, dass ich Fieber habe und ich mich einfach nicht wohl fühle.

Du ______________________________ (1P)

Ärztin Does anything hurt?

Du ______________________________ (1P)

Deine Mutter Ich habe Kopfschmerzen und mir ist kalt.

Du ______________________________ (1P)

Ärztin I see. When did it start?

Du ______________________________ (1P)

Deine Mutter Vor zwei Tagen, als ich auf einmal nichts essen konnte.

Du ______________________________ (2P)

Ärztin Well, I don't think it's anything serious. You should drink about two litres of water, fruit juice or tea every day. No coffee please. And don't stay in the sun too long.

Du ______________________________

______________________________ (2P)

Ärztin These pills should help you. Take one pill half an hour before every meal, three times a day. If you don't feel better in three days, I want to see you again.

Du ______________________________

______________________________ (2P)

Deine Mutter Vielen Dank.

Ärztin You're welcome. All the best.

WRITING

___ / 20

My trip to ...

Write about a city or town that you have visited. The city can be in Germany or in another country.

Write about the following things:
- when and why you went there
- who you went with
- what is important about the city
- what you did there
- what you liked/didn't like
- what your feelings and impressions were

Write about 120–140 words.

Texte schreiben
Die angegebenen Punkte geben dir bereits eine Struktur des Textes vor. Bevor du mit dem Schreiben beginnst, kannst du in einer Mindmap Ideen zu den einzelnen Punkten sammeln.

SPEAKING

___ / 16

Describing a photo

Look at the photo and describe it. Talk about the situation, the place, the time of day and the things you can see. What is the person in the photo doing and feeling?

New word
bonnet ['bɒnɪt] *Motorhaube*

Klassenarbeit B

Gesamtpunktzahl ohne Speaking _____ / 67 Note _____

Gesamtpunktzahl mit Speaking _____ / 87 Note _____

READING

_____ / 16

Leseverständnis üben
Sieh dir vor der Bearbeitung dieser Aufgabe noch einmal die Hinweise zum Reading im Skills File in deinem Englischbuch auf S. 144–145 an.

Life in South Africa today

We are three German students in year 9. At the moment we're doing some research for our end-of-year project on South Africa. We'd like to know what life is like in South Africa today after the end of apartheid. Any answers welcome.

Jule, Chrissi and Leander | 15 | Bremen, Germany

Hi, I'm David, I'm 15. Life has changed since the end of apartheid, but only for some people. Many people still have no jobs. For me life is still not good. I live with my mother, who is not working at the moment. I'd love to carry on with school but we haven't got enough money. I went to school till class eight but had to leave last year. Now I'm trying to find a job.

David | 15 | Mpumalanga, South Africa

I have my own little business. Enough to live off, you know. I mean, I'm not a rich person. What worries me really is crime. People break into people's houses and simply take what they can grab. Two weeks ago thieves broke into my house and took my TV set. The police don't care. I'm sad about this development.

Amanda | 36 | Western Cape, South Africa

I have worked as a farmer all my life. I used to live in a house with no water and no electricity. My situation has changed since my farm got a new owner. Now I have electricity and water and I even bought a second-hand computer last month. That's one of the results of the new government's work. It will still take a lot of time, but I am optimistic about my children's future. They won't have to live in poverty.

Jonathan | 42 | South Africa

II think that a lot has changed. Being a teacher in a township I can say that many things have improved. More kids can go to school, we have books for them and also some important equipment like TVs. Still, there are often 50 students in my class, and we have a high dropout rate. We're moving slowly towards a better future.

Dikeledi | 31 | Randburg

I'm 17 and I've just finished school. I only know about apartheid and the uprising from what my parents tell me. But I know that life was hard for black people then. Here in Jo'burg life has become very modern – with beautiful shopping centres, famous banks and great discos. Life is great here if you have enough money. My family isn't really rich, but I was able to go to school. Now I want to go on to university and study medicine. When my parents were my age that wasn't possible because of apartheid.

Kagiso | 17 | Johannesburg

a) *Write five things that have changed for the better since the end of apartheid.*
Write three things that still need to be changed for the better. (8P)

Things that have changed for the better:

____

____

____

____

____

Things that still need to be changed for the better:

____

____

b) *Now write around 50 words about how education in South Africa has changed since apartheid.*
Use your own words. (8P)

____

____

____

____

____

LANGUAGE

____ / 36

1 WORDS Combining words

____ / 10

a) *Combine the words from the boxes. Use each word only once. Sometimes you need to add* ***a*** *or* ***an****.* *(6P)*

send • rent • collect • fight for • fancy • hate

+

glamorous • official • crowded • small • political • impressive

+

autographs • message • flat • movie stars • trains • freedom

____

____

____

____

____

____

b) *Now use* ***four*** *combinations in meaningful sentences.* *(4P)*

____

____

____

____

2 WORDS Find the correct word

____/7

Complete the sentences with the correct words.

1 After the factory had closed, the ____________________ rate rose dramatically.

2 It's cheaper to use public ____________________ than to go by car.

3 In some places there is a lot of rubbish lying around – the places are ____________________.

4 I wasn't feeling well, so I went to the doctor. He gave me a ____________________ for some pills.

5 I met an old friend yesterday. He looked completely different, so I didn't ____________________ him first.

6 There were so many people who wanted to go to the concert. We had had to ____________________ for more than one hour before we got the tickets.

7 Can't we take the bus? I don't ____________________ walking all the way.

3 GRAMMAR I would have ...

____/5

a) *What would you have done differently? Make short dialogues. (4P)*

A I couldn't find my friend's house yesterday, so I wasn't able to take him the homework.

B (call him) I would have called him.

A I saw a man stealing a book in the bookshop, but I didn't do anything.

B ____ (tell the manager).

A When I was in London, I went to the British Museum.

B Museums are boring. ________________________________ (go to Madame Tussaud's).

A I saved all my pocket money and bought myself a new skateboard.

B ____ (buy surfboard).

A When I was 12 years old, I decided to learn Latin.

B ____ (decide to learn Spanish).

b) *Make **one** dialogue yourself and write it in your exercise book. (1P)*

4 GRAMMAR If ...

_____ / 8

Complete the sentences with the correct form of the if-clauses type 1, 2 or 3.

If-Sätze – Conditional sentences (type 1, 2 and 3)

Type 1	if-clause: **simple present**	main clause: **– will-future** **– can/should/must + Infinitiv**
	If I **go** to London,	I **will visit** Buckingham Palace.
	If she **wants** to do a sightseeing tour,	she **can take** the bus.
Type 2	if-clause: **simple past**	main clause: **would/could/might + Infinitiv**
	If my sister **went** to Australia,	she **would visit** Sydney.
	If I **wanted** to go to Australia,	I **would have to** book a flight very soon.
Type 3	if-clause: **past perfect**	main clause: **would/could + have + Partizip Perfekt**
	If Joanna **had seen** the red traffic light,	she **would have stopped**.
	If I **had gone** to the party,	I **could have danced** with Josh.

Schrittweises Vorgehen bei if-Sätzen

- Schreib dir zunächst die Regeln der 3 Arten der **if-Sätze** auf.
- Stelle dann fest, welcher Teil des **if-Satzes** vorgegeben ist und in welcher Zeit er steht.
- Im letzten Schritt kannst du dann die entsprechende Zeit bilden.

1 If Tom went to Australia for a year, his parents ______________________ (visit) him in the summer holidays.

2 If the Millers hadn't seen the advert for the house in the newspaper, they ______________________ (not move) to this beautiful area.

3 If the teacher tells us the date of our test, I ______________________ (start) preparing this afternoon.

4 Our cat Minca would be very unhappy if we ______________________ (leave) her alone over the weekend.

5 If the new student in our class ______________________ (talk) about his problems, my friend and I would have helped him.

6 If Susan ______________________ (not want) to study Spanish at university, she wouldn't go to Mexico for a year.

7 If I ______________________ (meet) John this afternoon, I will ask him about the project.

8 The three boys wouldn't have started fighting if the others ______________________ (leave) them alone.

5 GRAMMAR If, if, if ...

_____ / 6

a) *Read the sentences, then circle the right answer. (3P)*

1 John, if you take these pills, you'll be OK again by Sunday.

Can John get well by Sunday? Yes / No

2 Susan, if you had come just five minutes earlier, you would have met Uncle Rick.

Did Susan meet Uncle Rick? Yes / No

3 Alan, if you follow the instructions carefully, you will be able to install the telephone quickly.

Can he install the telephone quickly? Yes / No

b) *Read the sentences, then tick the right answer. (3P)*

1 If the students stay quiet, ...	a) the teacher wouldn't have given them any homework.	
	b) the teacher will not give them any homework.	

2 If the Millers moved from Bristol to London, ...	a) Cindy would live in London.	
	b) Cindy would have lived in London.	

3 If I had left home a bit earlier, ...	a) I will catch the bus.	
	b) I would have caught the bus.	

MEDIATION

____/15

A conversation about Berlin public transport

Während eines Urlaubs lernt deine Familie Herrn und Frau Gonzales, ein spanisches Ehepaar, kennen. Die beiden möchten in einigen Wochen Berlin besuchen. Deine Eltern kennen Berlin sehr gut und geben Auskunft über den öffentlichen Nahverkehr. Du hilfst mit der englischen Sprache.

Frau Gonzales We're flying to Berlin-Schönefeld. How do we get to the city centre from the airport?

Du ______________________________

______________________________ (2P)

Deine Mutter Am besten nehmen sie die S-Bahn. Wo ist denn ihr Hotel?

Du ______________________________

______________________________ (2P)

Herr Gonzales I think it's right in the city centre at a square called "Alexanderplatz". Do you know it?

Du ______________________________

______________________________ (2P)

Dein Vater Natürlich kenne ich den. Das ist sehr gut, denn man kann direkt mit der S-Bahn dorthin fahren und man braucht überhaupt nicht umsteigen.

Du ______________________________

______________________________ (3P)

Frau Gonzales That's fine. Now what about the tickets? Where do we get them and how much are they?

Du ______________________________ (2P)

Dein Vater Am besten kauft man die Fahrscheine schon vorher übers Internet. Es gibt besondere Tickets für Touristen, die 2, 3 oder 5 Tage genutzt werden können.
Man kann dann fahren so oft man will, sogar bis nach Potsdam.

Du ______________________________

____

____

____

______________________________ (4P)

Herr Gonzales That's great. Thank you so much for your information. I think it's time for a cup of coffee. Come on.

SPEAKING

____/ 20

13 My holidays

Some students present their holidays in class. Listen to Moritz.

Write down the outline and the visual material he uses in his presentation. Then note useful phrases that can be helpful when you are giving a presentation. Use the table below for your notes.

Outline + visual material	Useful phrases

Eine Präsentation halten
Zur Bearbeitung dieser Aufgabe kannst du dir das Skills File in deinem Englischbuch auf S. 139 noch einmal ansehen.

Now you

Prepare a short talk about your holidays or a school trip.
Think of an outline and collect ideas for every point you want to make. Collect some visual materials that will make your presentation more interesting and easier to understand.
You can collect your ideas in this mind map:

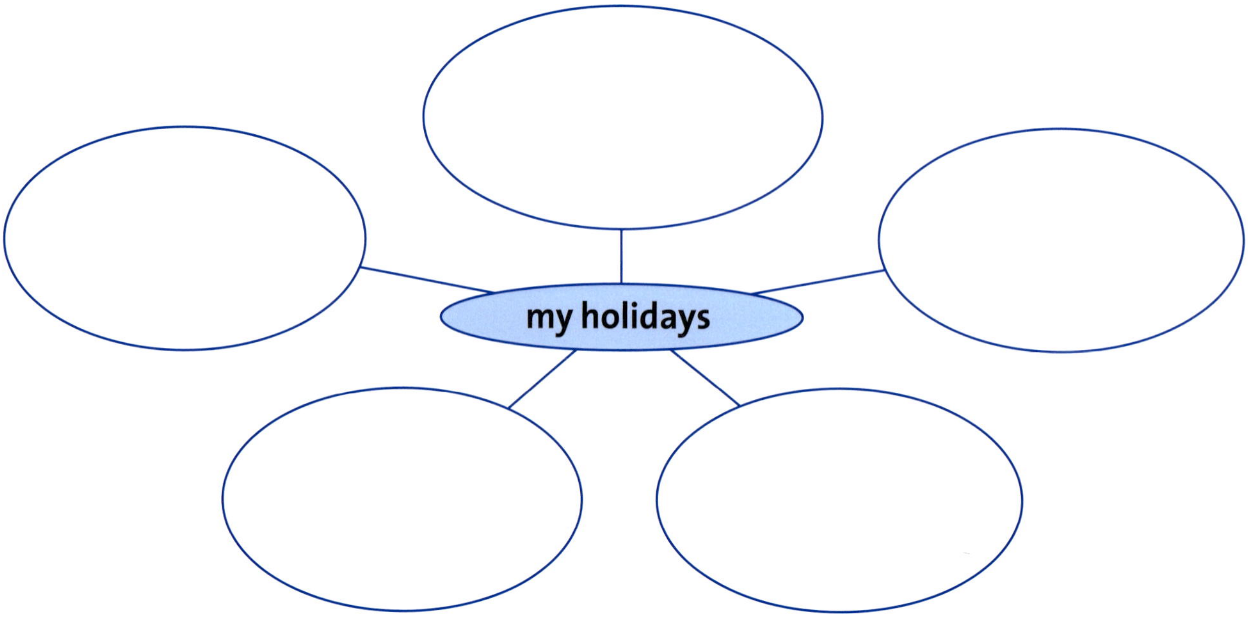

How to do well in a test

Countdown zum Testerfolg

Ein Test ist angekündigt? Kein Grund zur Panik. Wichtig ist, dass du weißt, worauf du dich vorbereiten musst. Im Zweifelsfall frag deine Lehrerin oder deinen Lehrer. Der Countdown kann beginnen!

Eine Woche vor dem Test

1 Lies noch einmal die **Texte** der zuletzt durchgenommenen Unit (A-Section und Text, eventuell auch das Background File). Fasse mündlich oder schriftlich zusammen, worum es ging.

2 Wiederhole den **Wortschatz** der Unit mit Hilfe des *Vocabulary* oder des *Wordmaster*. Schreibe dir die Wörter und Wortverbindungen, die du immer wieder vergisst, auf ein Blatt Papier. Eine Mindmap oder ein Wortfeld helfen beim Behalten.

3 Geh auch noch mal die neue **Grammatik** durch. Aufgaben zur Selbstüberprüfung und zum Üben findest du im *Practice*-Teil, auf der Seite „How am I doing?", im *Grammar File* (S. 158–169), in deinem *Workbook* und im *e-Workbook*.

Zwei Tage vor dem Test

1 Wiederhole den **Wortschatz**. Manche Wörter sitzen noch nicht? Schreibe einen kurzen Text, in dem du sie verwendest.

2 Lies die **Texte** ein weiteres Mal.

3 Erkläre einem Freund oder einer Freundin die neue **Grammatik**. Das klappt nicht richtig? Dann lies nochmal im *Grammar File* nach.

Am Abend vor dem Test

1 Entspanne dich. Du kannst lesen, dich in die Badewanne legen, Musik hören, fernsehen, ...

2 Geh zur gewohnten Zeit ins Bett.

Am Morgen des Tests

1 Steh rechtzeitig auf, damit du nicht hetzen musst.

2 Lies irgendetwas „zum Aufwärmen", aber schau nicht mehr in dein Schülerbuch.

Während des Tests

1 Denk daran: Du hast dich gut vorbereitet. Es gibt keinen Grund, nervös zu sein.

2 Konzentriere dich auf den Test, lass dich nicht ablenken.

3 Lies dir die Aufgaben genau durch. Dann löse zuerst die Aufgaben, die dir einfach scheinen. Wende dich erst danach den schwereren Aufgaben zu.

4 Aufgaben, die du bearbeitet hast, hakst du ab. So siehst du, wie du vorankommst, und behältst den Überblick.

5 Schau ab und zu auf die Uhr. Du solltest dir für den Schluss noch etwas Zeit einplanen, um deine Antworten noch einmal durchzulesen und wenn nötig zu korrigieren.

Aufgabenstellungen verstehen

Bevor du anfängst, die Aufgaben zu bearbeiten, vergewissere dich, dass du genau weißt, was du tun sollst. Lies die Aufgabe Wort für Wort langsam und gründlich und von Anfang bis Ende durch. Du kannst besonders wichtige Teile der Aufgabenstellung unterstreichen und die Aufgabe, wenn nötig, für dich in einzelne Schritte unterteilen.

Den folgenden Arbeitsanweisungen begegnest du häufig:

Add Verbinde eine Information oder einen Sachverhalt mit einer/einem anderen auf die geforderte Art und Weise.

Choose Wähle zwischen verschiedenen Möglichkeiten die passende Information aus.

Comment Kommentiere einen Sachverhalt durch die Darstellung deiner eigenen Meinung dazu. Begründe und erläutere sie möglichst genau.

Compare Vergleiche Dinge, Wörter oder Sachverhalte, indem du prüfst, ob und auf welche Weise sie gleiche oder verschiedene Eigenschaften, Aussehen, Bedeutungen oder Funktionen haben.

Complete Ergänze eine Information, indem du sie an dem dafür vorgesehenen Platz einträgst und damit z. B. einen Satz sinnvoll beendest.

Describe Beschreibe ein Objekt oder eine Person, d.h. stelle dar, wie sie aussehen, wie das Objekt funktioniert oder die Personen handeln. Vermeide eigene Wertungen wie z. B. „beautiful", „useful" oder „great".

Discuss Diskutiere ein Thema, eine Behauptung oder eine Aussage. Untersuche möglichst viele Seiten davon, z. B. Vor- und Nachteile, und stelle diese geordnet dar.

Explain Erkläre einen Sachverhalt, d. h. gib wesentliche Fakten über ihn und erläutere, wie sie logisch zusammenhängen.

Fill in Trage die geforderten Informationen in den dafür vorgesehenen Platz ein, z. B. in eine Lücke oder eine Tabelle.

List Schreibe einzelne oder mehrere Informationen übersichtlich und geordnet auf, z. B. in einer Reihe, Tabelle oder einem anderen Verzeichnis.

Listen Höre dir einen Text, einzelne Informationen oder Sachverhalte an.

Match Ordne die angegebenen Informationen einander zu, wie es die Aufgabe erfordert. Finde z. B. Satzanfänge und passende Satzenden und füge sie zusammen.

Use Verwende eine Tatsache, ein Wort usw. so, wie es in der Aufgabe gefordert wird.

Write a ... Schreibe etwas in einem geforderten Textformat auf, z. B. deinen Kommentar zu etwas oder eine Geschichte.